MORE
GROWING UP
CATHOLIC

MORE
GROWING UP
CATHOLIC

MARY JANE FRANCES CAVOLINA MEARA
JEFFREY ALLEN JOSEPH STONE
MAUREEN ANNE TERESA KELLY
RICHARD GLEN MICHAEL DAVIS

ILLUSTRATIONS BY
BOB KILEY

A DOLPHIN BOOK
DOUBLEDAY & COMPANY, INC.
GARDEN CITY, NEW YORK

This Dolphin Books edition is the first publication of
More Growing Up Catholic.

Copyright © 1986 by Jane Cavolina Meara, Jeffrey A. Stone,
Maureen A. Kelly and Richard G. Davis

Designed by Bernard Schleifer
Produced by East Chelsea Press

PHOTOGRAPHY CREDITS: AP/Wide World Photos: *pages 13, 37, 49, 51, 61, 89,*
98, 110. Laura Worsham: *pages 44, 66, 67, 68, 99, 100, 101, 102, 117.*
Alinari/Art Resource: *pages 84, 112, 123.* Scala/Art Resource: *page 124.*

Library of Congress Cataloging-in-Publication Data

More growing up Catholic.

"A Dolphin book."
1. Catholic Church—Anecdotes, facetiae, satire, etc.
I. Meara, Mary Jane Frances Cavolina, 1954–
BX1755.M66   1986   282   86-9025
ISBN 0-385-23665-4

To Stella Dick, and to Herbert Merlin;
To Greg, Liz, Ted, and Sue;
To Mary Mersnik, and to Anne, Kevin, Claire,
Patrick, Vincent, and Liam;
To Donald and Rita Davis

ACKNOWLEDGMENTS

THE ASSISTANCE OF friends, colleagues, and family members was not only valued, but essential, in the preparation of this book. Many thanks are owed to the following people:

Loretta Barrett, for her professionalism, editorial guidance, and faith in our idea; Elaine Markson and Geri Thoma, for their unflagging support, patience, and enthusiasm; Patrick Filley, for his much-appreciated efforts; Felecia Abbadessa; Mary McCarthy and Cynthia Barrett.

Laura Worsham, for the original photographs, and her models: George Coleman, Jim Fitzgerald, Chick Foxgrover, Amy Freitag, Henry Hirsch, and Bill Scovin.

Thanks also to Bernard Schleifer, for his care in the design of the book; and to Pauline Piekarz, for copyediting.

For their unfailing friendship, support, enthusiasm, and help: Fr. William Belford, Deborah Berardi, Fran Black, Msgr. Casey, Doug Cassidy, Fr. A. J. Chandonnet, Ty Danco, Sr. Catherine Devilly, Stephen Geiger, Howie Greenberg, Tom Hill, Wilma and Ed Hodakievic, Sarah McKenzie Hoskins, Maria Lepore Hunsicker, Barry Kaiser, Judy Koerner, John Lepore, Lou Lepore, Greg Lester, Carol Livingston, Fr. James Hart McCown, S. J., Beth Martin, Sr. Mary Jo, Kathy Matthews, Joe Mersnik, Peter Mertens, Mary and Mike Monks, Chris and David Patin, Becca Peterson, Sandy Radnovich, Ashley Rogers, Lottie Shivers, Kathy Flaherty Smith, Amy Bass Wilson, Mary Ann Woodward, Dr. Antoinette Ambrosino Wyszynski, John Zaborski.

For invaluable advice the following friends in publishing: Andy Ambraziejus, Deborah Broide, Howard Cady, Mary Coffey, Lisa Drew, Michele Farinet, Anne Kostick, Jim Landis, Larry Norton, Jennifer Rogers, Meg Ruley, Bert Snyder, Peter Workman, Andi Zipper.

Finally, our families, who once again were there whenever we needed them, and then some: Shirley and Frank Cavolina; Ellen, Lisa, Robbie, Larry, Lorraine, Michael, Joan, Jason, Jessica, Julie, Jeremy, and Krista; Brian Meara; Charlie and Ethel Meara and the Meara/Murphy clan; Donald and Rita Davis; Steven and Cindy Davis; Tom, Sharon, Sean, and Ryan Carroll; Don, Eileen, Donny, and John Davis; Jackie Kourim and family; the Kelly family; Anne and Norman Stone, the rest of the Stones, the Strachs, and the Flahertys.

CONTENTS

ONE
POOR BANISHED
CHILDREN OF EVE

TWO
THE SALT OF
THE EARTH

THREE
POVERTY, CHASTITY, AND OBEDIENCE

FOUR
UPON THIS ROCK

FIVE
ALL THINGS VISIBLE
AND INVISIBLE

INTRODUCTION

More Growing Up Catholic, like *Growing Up Catholic,* is for every Catholic, whether devout, practicing, lapsed, or excommunicated. Wherever you happened to grow up—in Portland, Maine, or Portland, Oregon, in Toronto or Texas—you share with millions of other Catholics the indelible marks of a shared heritage.

In *Growing Up Catholic,* we covered everything from the *Baltimore Catechism* to Guardian Angels to giving up chocolate for Lent. Still, even as we finished writing *Growing Up Catholic,* it was apparent that there were many important topics that would have to be left out. After all, how could anyone possibly deal with 2,000 years of Roman Catholicism in one slim volume?

We began to keep a list of subjects we hadn't yet addressed, meanwhile praying that the response to *Growing Up Catholic* would be favorable enough to warrant *More Growing Up Catholic.* But we weren't quite prepared for the warmth and enthusiasm of that response. We were flattered to hear that priests quoted from *Growing Up Catholic* in their sermons. At least one Cardinal mentioned it in church, and we like to think that maybe even the Pope sneaked a peek.

Most of all, however, we were gratified to find that Regular Catholics like ourselves enjoyed reading our book, and that it helped to stir up their own memories. We hope that *More Growing Up Catholic* does the same.

ONE

POOR BANISHED CHILDREN OF EVE

A DAY IN THE LIFE OF A PAROCHIAL SCHOOL CHILD

8:15 A.M.   Bell

8:15.5 A.M.   Children silently line up in front of their class-rooms—boys in one line, girls in another, shortest to tallest, one arm's length apart.

8:16 A.M.   Hands over hearts, the children say the Pledge of Allegiance as the flag is raised. They are grateful to live in the land of the free and the home of the brave.

8:19 A.M.   No, there are no crickets on the playground. It's Sister with her clicker. Each line marches into a class-room.

8:20 A.M.   Informal inspection by Sister. Uniforms spotless? Socks pulled up? Fingernails clean? Giggle potential high.

8:25 A.M.   Morning prayers. Just one decade of the Rosary this morning. Shannon Ryan forgets her Rosary and has to borrow one from Sister.

8:35 A.M.   Religion. Pop quiz on questions from the *Baltimore Catechism*. No one can explain the Eighth Commandment. Sister looks peevish.

9:15 A.M.   Arithmetic. "If three loaves and five fishes were multiplied five hundredfold, how many of each would there be?"

10:00 A.M.   Sister's clicker clicks. Recess. The sole purpose of recess is to allow children to use the bathroom. They are permitted to talk at will, and revel in their freedom.

10:15 A.M.   Back to the classroom for a quick Our Father, Hail Mary, and Glory Be.

10:20 A.M.   Science. Sister explains the root systems of vegetables as her students insert celery stalks in beakers of colored water. All vegetables are gifts from God.

11:00 A.M.   Surprise visit from Father! Everyone sits up straight and Sister beams and wipes the chalk dust off her hands. Father discusses vocations, and by the time he leaves everyone thinks that maybe they do have the calling.

11:55 A.M.   Sister's clicker clicks and all rise to say Grace Before Meals.

12:00 noon   Lunchtime. It's hot dog day! The cafeteria ladies also serve beans, cole slaw and half-pints of whole milk. David Cooney eats four hot dogs and has to go to the nurse's office.

12:30 P.M.	Recess. Boys practice hoops. Girls jump rope. Sister reprimands "roughhousers."
1:00 P.M.	Recess ends. Lines file back into classrooms. Sister leads Grace After Meals.
1:03 P.M.	Social Studies. The class reads about Kara and Jimi, island children who live in the South Seas. Kara and Jimi are not Catholic. That is why we must support the mission.

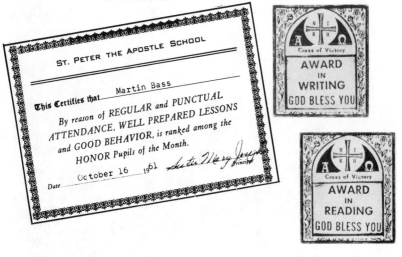

ST. PETER THE APOSTLE SCHOOL

This Certifies that _____ Martin Bass _____

By reason of REGULAR and PUNCTUAL ATTENDANCE, WELL PREPARED LESSONS and GOOD BEHAVIOR, is ranked among the HONOR Pupils of the Month.

Date _____ October 16 _____ 1961 _____ Sister Mary Joseph, Principal

Cross of Victory
AWARD IN WRITING
GOD BLESS YOU

Cross of Victory
AWARD IN READING
GOD BLESS YOU

1:30 P.M.	Spelling. Today's spelling bee includes the words "transubstantiation," "Confiteor" and "monstrance."
2:00 P.M.	P.E. Gym shorts have been worn under uniforms, so boys remove their pants, girls their jumpers. Teams are picked and a vicious game of kickball ensues. Liz Evans falls and chips her front tooth.
3:00 P.M.	Uniforms back on. One more decade of the Rosary to end the day.
3:15 P.M.	Final bell rings. Orderly exit from classroom under Sister's watchful eye, but flight through schoolyard resembles scene from *Wild in the Streets*. Joyous din can be heard for blocks.

IN GOD'S HOUSE

CATHOLIC SCHOOLCHILDREN spend half their lives in church. The hour on Sunday that generates weeping and wailing from adults is only a drop in a very big bucket for parochials. In the life of a Catholic schoolchild, Mass can take place at any time and for almost any reason. Witness the Graduation Mass, the Opening-of-School Mass, or, worst of all, the Somebody-Important-Died Mass. If that Important Somebody happened to be a priest or a nun, or, God forbid, a Monsignor, you were in for an affair that made *Gone with the Wind* look like a short subject.

But the Masses that were being said for *you* were far and away the most rigorous, and for many good reasons. First of all, you knew you didn't really have to be there. The Guy in Charge had not asked/demanded your presence; no mortal sin would appear on the clean milk bottle that was your soul if you didn't appear. But since this type of Mass usually took place during school hours, getting out of Alcatraz would have been easier than getting out of going.

Secondly, you knew that Sister was making an enormous sac-

rifice for you. After all, she'd given up *everything* in life just to teach you, and she was taking time away from the most important thing in the world to pray for your unworthy, and usually ungrateful, soul. You knew that anything that got you excused from school was Mighty Important. This knowledge demanded extra holiness.

Lastly, this was one of the few occasions when your demeanor at Mass was being closely scrutinized by the Blackskirts. If their inspection revealed one turn of the head, one yawn, or the tiniest little whisper to your neighbor (who was, after all, seated a foot away, next to the space you left for your Guardian Angel), you were ruined.

The runner-up to Mass for time-in-church consumption was rehearsal. Catholic schoolchildren rehearsed for everything—processions, First Holy Communion, Graduation, Confirmation, and sundry other rituals—several times. The process of lining the class up in size order alone could take hours. And once that was accomplished, we rehearsed walking down the aisle at just the right pace and with just the right amount of space between ourselves and the person in front of us, stopping at the pew assigned to us, genuflecting, entering the pew, moving to the spot in the pew assigned to us, kneeling down, and staying motionless until Sister's clicker told us we were all in place and could sit. Since one absolutely did not turn one's head from the altar, if Sister had not signaled to us by clicking or clapping, we would be kneeling still. These rehearsals were enlivened when singing was part of the program.

Although this came around only seasonally, the all-around fave reason for being herded into church was to say the Stations of the Cross each Friday in Lent. Cried at *Kramer vs. Kramer?* Despondent over Paul McCartney's marriage? *Nothing* in life could match the Stations for high drama, pathos, and overall catharsis. Particularly sympathetic sobs were heard when the altar boy intoned, "Veronica wipes the face of Jesus." She was a Regular Person. It could have been *us.* And haughty indignation was rampant as Jesus fell three times. If we had been there, we would have helped Him.

Altar boys were in a class by themselves in the time-in-church sweepstakes. In addition to their duties at Sunday Masses and on Holy Days of Obligation, altar boys served at Nuptial Masses, put in time before school began (serving predawn Masses attended only by the frighteningly pious), and were frequently released from class to serve weekday Funeral Masses.

THE FIRST TIME I SAW VELCRO

AN ALTAR BOY'S STORY

THE GREATEST PRIVILEGE bestowed upon an altar boy, along with the lesser privileges of learning Latin and ringing the chimes, is access to that holy of holies, the sacristy. Although we had made numerous forays to the steps of the altar in learning our routine for the celebration of Mass, we had never actually been in this hallowed space. I mean, *nobody* gets to go back there except the priests and the people who clean up. I will always remember those first tentative steps into the quietude of the room behind the altar. The scent was heavenly, a mixture of incense and fine wine.

It was customary for one of the more seasoned altar boys to be paired with a rookie for his first Mass. As I waited in the deafening quiet of the sacristy for Joey Potek, I snuck a peek at the many wonders it held.

The gold-plated candle snuffer rested against a cabinet that held the censer and many small black cakes of charcoal. I took a quick look over at the priest's side of the sacristy to make sure I was alone, surreptitiously lit a match, and placed it against one of the pieces of charcoal. "What are you doing, you dip!" Joey Potek's voice boomed out. "Just practicing," I lied weakly.

"Come on, Ding-Dong, we gotta get dressed," he testily shot back. He opened a large wooden closet filled with what seemed to me to be hundreds of black cassocks and frilly white surplices in every shape and style. "Which one do I wear?" I asked, my voice shaking. "Whichever one will fit you, dork," he helpfully offered.

Joey Potek threw his cassock on, grabbed a surplice, and beat it for the priest's side of the sacristy. I was left alone in front of the wardrobe. With sweaty palms, I tried on two or three

cassocks. The first was too long, the second was high water, but the third was just right.

I could hear the priest rattling around on his side, and the mumbled Eddie Haskell–style responses of Joey Potek to the priest. I knew it was getting close to the time we should be starting, but I was far from properly attired. I reached for the buttons and was horrified to find in their place a strip of scratchy material running along the length of the garment.

Nearly in tears, I sheepishly proceeded to the priest's side and was met with two sets of disapproving eyes. "How do you do this?" I blurted out, holding the open front of the cassock and demonstrating the lack of buttons. "It's Velcro, you jerk," Joey Potek hissed as he pressed the two strips together on the front of my gown. The rest of the Mass was a haze to me, although the priest later said that I had done a very good job. But to this day, whenever I see Velcro strips on anything, I get a queasy feeling.

ALTAR BOY'S WARDROBE

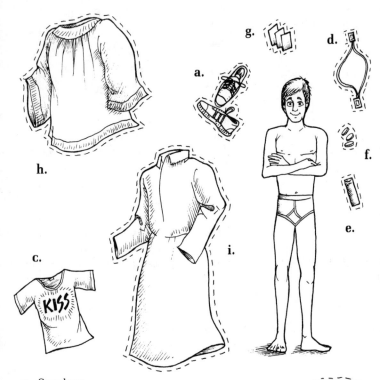

a. Sneakers

b. Cut-off jeans

c. T-shirt with picture of heavy-metal rock group

d. Scapular awarded for year's service as altar boy

e. Candy bar to break fast after Mass

f. Change left over from buying candy bar

g. Mixed pack of holy cards and baseball cards

h. Surplice—loose white knee-length vestment with large open sleeves, worn by altar boys and sometimes choir members

i. Cassock—ankle-length robe, usually black, with close-fitting sleeves; worn under surplice at Mass

ALTAR BOY FAVES AND TURNOFFS

Compiled by *The Little Server*, the Magazine of Altar Boys

Faves

Holding the paten. And watching how gross everyone's tongue looks when they stick it out to receive the host.

Serving the priest the water and the wine. First experience dealing with fine crystal; could prepare one for a career in a three-star restaurant.

Ringing the bells. Develops sense of rhythm; many rock drummers were once altar boys.

Helping the priest put on his chasuble. Good training for future man Friday.

Lighting the incense. First experience with exotic fragrances and matches. Excellent background for a member of the counterculture.

Turnoffs

Serving 6:00 A.M. Mass. No one except farmers should be made to get up this early.

Serving 10:30 A.M. Mass. Since this Mass usually features the choir, it can run fifteen to twenty minutes longer than the regular Mass.

Serving Funeral Mass. Depressing and spooky.

Serving Wedding Mass. A lot of work for not much return if bridegroom is not generous with tip.

Serving Christmas Midnight Mass. Drippy candles and drunks.

ALTAR BOY FUN

1. When friends step up to receive Communion, "slice" their throats with the paten. *Do not* draw blood (a venial sin), but try to come close.

2. Swipe a pocketful of unconsecrated hosts from the sacristy after Mass.

3. When you're kneeling next to the altar boy who's in charge of ringing the bells, nudge him at odd intervals. If he's daydreaming, he'll immediately snap to and jangle the bells. Ha-ha.

4. Swing the censer as hard as you can to emit as much incense as possible. See how many people cough and fan themselves.

5. Just for fun, wear only your swimsuit under your cassock.

FOR GOD AND MONEY

"Hi, we're selling these chocolate bars to raise money for new basketball hoops at Holy Name. Do you want to buy some?"

EVERY YEAR, in every parochial school in every diocese, funds must be raised for overhead projectors, a new science lab, or a couch for the teachers' lounge. Because parochial school administrators are firm believers in the door-to-door philosophy of raising money, it's up to the kids themselves to do the legwork.

The children accept their role as hucksters with innocence, but after a couple of selling sprees, the holy peddlers fall into categories represented by these children:

Lazy: Michele sells a couple of Holy Childhood Christmas Seals to her older sister, then loses interest. If her parents don't care whether she helps support the school that is giving her an education far superior to what a public school can offer, no one can *make* her sell. But the nuns will remember.

Obedient: If Bob is told to sell magazine subscriptions every day after school in the snow, then that's what he'll do. He feels almost guilty accepting the free subscription to *Catholic Digest* that he is awarded for making ten sales.

Zealous: Another chance to be the best! Meg is a competitive overachiever who thrives on challenge. She likes nothing better than stalking the streets in search of potential holiday fruitcake buyers. She will eventually make millions selling real estate and will donate generous sums to the Church in thanksgiving for her invaluable training.

Pagan Babies We Didn't Buy

Feeling guilty about that last Chunky? The pack of baseball cards you had to have? Well, you should be. 'Cause if we had all been better children, if we had put just a little more money in our mission boxes, we could have bought more pagan babies. Here's a list of some of the ones we didn't get to:

Muammar al-Qaddafi
Ayatollah Khomeini
Yasir Arafat
Tokyo Rose
Mikhail Gorbachev
Bhagwan Shree Rajneesh

"You've got a lot to live and St. Scholastica has a lot to give."

A WORD FROM THE PRINCIPAL

Another successful school year has ended, but for you life has only just begun. No more this year will the halls resound with the sound of slamming lockers, but for you life has just begun. No more will the sound of boys joyously practicing football (and offering their pain up to Our Lord) cascade across the playing field, but for you life has just begun. No more will the angelic sound of our girls' voices raised in prayer drift through these sacred corridors, but for you life has just begun. New directions, new challenges, new sounds are just over the horizon. Indeed, for you, life has just begun.

—Sr. Thomas Anne

SENIORS

For our seniors, this has been a most rewarding year. A year of growth, a year of trial. For some, it's on to college. For others, it's back to their jobs at the gas station or the White Castle. Still others will enlist in the military, and a few lucky ones will play basketball for nationally ranked Catholic colleges. But no matter what their destination, they will carry with them the values instilled in them by a Catholic education—the best education in the world.

Seniors, remember you are representatives of St. Scholastica High School.

Mary Ann-Margaret Antobelli

Sodality, Glee Club, Student Council, *Horizons,* Homeroom President, Future Nuns, Retreat Club

"Mary" . . . Loves long walks on the beach, praying, and pizza . . . Hates liars and phony people . . . Favorite saint: Mary . . . Happiness is macaroni and cheese and going to church . . . Can be seen in the chapel at all hours . . . "I don't find that funny at all."

Patrick John Crawford

Liturgy Club, Basketball, Baseball, Swimming, Bowling, Future Priests, Poster Club, Retreat Club

"Pat" . . . Loves Marquette basketball, flirting, and black clothes . . . Hates pizza . . . Favorite saint: Patrick . . . Happiness is a backward lay-up and new gym clothes . . . "Nice shot!"

Frank Czussazak
Wrestling, Junior Janitors

"Scuz" . . . Loves Top Job and a pail of warm water . . . Hates the English language . . . Favorite saint: Petro of Dzaab . . . Happiness is a clean floor with all the scraps of paper picked up . . . "What you say?"

Mary Ellen Fastenelli
Bowling

"Fast Mary" . . . Loves hair spray and the backseats of '57 Chevys . . . Hates school and her parents . . . Favorite saint: Mary Magdalene . . . Happiness is sleeping late and Saturdays . . . "Bug off."

Joseph Hamilton
Thespians, Catholic Communicators Club, *Horizons, Weekly Scholar*

"Ham" . . . Loves Eugene O'Neill and Eugene Ionesco . . . Hates jocks and pep rallies . . . Favorite saint: Joseph . . . Happiness is meeting people and seeing a Broadway show . . . Would like to go to Europe . . . Digs Andrew Greeley . . . "To be or not to be."

Katherine Kelly
Sodality, Home Economics Club, Future Housekeepers, Junior Decorators

"Mrs. K." . . . Loves cooking and cleaning and ironing on rainy days . . . Hates going outside and doing anything "too exciting" . . . Favorite saint: Hazel . . . Happiness is making a really big pot of goulash and having people eat it . . . "Hungry?"

ST. SCHOLASTICA CLUBS AND ORGANIZATIONS

DENTED CAN CLUB

One of the oldest of the service clubs at St. Scholastica, their cry is, "Don't throw that dented can away. We can use it!" The annual relief effort for inner-city residents was a smashing success, with 202 cans of cling peaches collected in one week.

L. to R.:
Mr. Heinz, Moderator; M. Van Camp, Secretary; C. Stokeley, President; V. Del Monte, Vice-President; P. Campbell, Treasurer

COOKING CLUB

The annual Cooking Club dinner was a great success this year. The menu included St. Basil Soup, St. Sebastian Cabbage, and Roast Beef Jogues. Here are two members of the club sampling the fare before the big dinner.

L. Mary Homemaker, *R.* Mary Kitchen

FUTURE CATHOLIC BASKETBALLERS OF AMERICA

The finest examples of Catholic boyhood in our school, these members of the frosh, soph, and varsity teams intend to "spread the word" while pursuing careers in Catholic basketball at our nation's fine Catholic colleges. All former CYO players, these hoopsmen have all earned basketball scholarships to their individual pledge schools.

Clockwise from top left:
S. Lam, Marquette; D. Unk, Georgetown; D. D. Dribble, St. John's; Billy "The Little Truth" Tyler, Villanova; Earl Pearl, Notre Dame; Perry "The Refrigerator" Williams, De Paul; S. S. Minnow, Providence

ASSISI SOCIETY

The Assisi Society is a national organization of high school students who pursue careers in the field of animal husbandry or veterinary medicine while simultaneously preparing to become monks. We are proud to announce that our candidate for the Assisi Society, Fred Furlip, has been accepted at the Monastery of the Little Creatures in Burr, South Dakota.

Fred says, "I've always liked going out in the woods and walking around till I got lost and then praying real hard till I found my way home." Asked if the cloistered life might be a little

lonely, Fred says, "I don't like talking to other people all that much anyway. Except for God, of course."

HOLY SCHOOL SPIRIT
PROFILES OF CATHOLIC COLLEGES

University of Notre Dame. Notre Dame, Indiana.
First Catholic university to achieve immortality (Hollywood-style, that is), in the 1940 movie *Knute Rockne: All American,* in which "the Gipper" was played by you-know-who. Until recently, indisputably the best-known Catholic college in America. Campus landmarks include large artworks with biblical themes, familiarly known as "Touchdown Jesus" and "First Down Moses." Notre Dame sports in the past few years ain't what they used to be, though, and East Coast rival Georgetown is making a strong bid for academic and athletic preeminence. Still, you can always tell Notre Dame alums by the "God Made ND #1" bumper stickers plastered all over their cars.

St. Mary's College. Notre Dame, Indiana.
The women at this small liberal arts school used to have a near-monopoly on Notre Dame men until the Fighting Irish went coed. With men continuing to outnumber women at Notre Dame, however, the "Smicks," as they are fondly known, still stand a fighting chance. Either way, Notre Dame men are provided with Suitable Catholic Mates.

Georgetown University. Washington, D.C.
Oldest, preppiest, most expensive Catholic college in America. Also in danger of becoming the most famous, owing to Patrick Ewing and company, celebrity alums (Maria Shriver), and internationally known faculty members (Jeane Kirkpatrick). Also, stairs on campus used in filming scene in *The Exorcist.* Ironically, because of Ewing, inner-city youngsters now sport blue Hoya silks in some of the poorest neighborhoods in America. Appropriately, Georgetown was chosen as the setting for the film *St. Elmo's Fire.* If the Brat Pack deigned to attend college, they would fit in perfectly here.

College of the Holy Cross. Worcester, Massachusetts.
The first Catholic college in New England, Holy Cross was found-

ed in 1843 as an alternative to a socially exclusive, Protestant educational establishment. It quickly became a socially exclusive Catholic educational establishment. Students bear four years at "the Cross" by studying hard, abusing alcohol, and escaping from Worcester as often as possible.

Boston College. Chestnut Hill, Massachusetts.

Like Holy Cross, Boston College started out as an alternative—not to the Protestants, but to Holy Cross. Originally located in the slums of Boston's South End, BC set out to serve the sons of immigrants who couldn't afford a gentleman's education. But the College quickly moved up in the world and out to the tony suburbs, eventually surpassing intrastate rival Holy Cross in size and athletic prowess. Former BC quarterback Doug Flutie was noted for giving new meaning to the term "Hail Mary pass."

Spring Hill College. Mobile, Alabama.

Rumor has it that this school of just over 1,000 has more than enough room for every Catholic college student from the Deep South. A good choice for those who desire a Jesuit education in a country club atmosphere, complete with the scent of magnolia and traditional Southern college high jinks.

College of New Rochelle. New Rochelle, New York.

Women's college in suburban New York dedicated to producing Suitable Catholic Mates for men at nearby Iona.

Iona College. New Rochelle, New York.

Excellent basketball teams allow for sublimation of sexual energies until Suitable Catholic Mate is selected from nearby College of New Rochelle. Founded by the Irish Christian Brothers.

Fordham University. Manhattan and Bronx, New York.

Fordham has two campuses—the original one in midtown Manhattan next to Lincoln Center, the other—wistfully known as Rose Hill—in the Bronx. The Lincoln Center campus offers ready access to arts and communications facilities; Rose Hill provides continuing informal instruction in street combat techniques.

St. John's University. Queens and Staten Island, New York.

Catholic higher education in the Outer Boroughs of New York City, courtesy of the Vincentian Fathers. Traditionally Fordham's big sports rival, lately St. John's has been hunting for bigger game, such as Georgetown and Villanova. Proud alums include Mario Cuomo, Governor of New York, and George Deukmejian, Governor of California.

Providence College. Providence, Rhode Island.

Well-supported and well-regarded Dominican institution in the most Catholic state in the Union (66%). Integral part of Little Rhody's old-boy network. To the great satisfaction of PC students, perennially strong hockey and basketball teams regularly trounce crosstown Ivy League rival Brown.

Villanova University. Villanova, Pennsylvania.

Villanova students traditionally have been great runners, garnering numerous major championships in men's and women's indoor and outdoor track, as well as cross country. Lately they've been playing superb basketball as well, bringing home the national college crown in 1985. Located on Philadelphia's wealthy Main Line, Villanova is adjacent to an Augustinian seminary, making it a convenient choice for students who think they may have the calling.

Rosemont College. Rosemont, Pennsylvania.

This tiny (650-student) women's college is more than a source of dates for men at nearby Villanova and St. Joseph's. Founded by an Episcopalian lady who later became a Catholic nun, the College accepts young women of good family and turns out highly motivated achievers.

The Newman Club: Home Away from Home

After twelve uniformed years of Catholic education, some students will decide to forgo the experience of attending a Catholic college. Fortunately, just about every college and university has a Newman Club, which Catholic collegians are encouraged to join.

Many Clubs are full-scale, well-organized parishes, replete with "modern art" religious banners on the walls and social events that are quite unlike the CYO dances back home. The priests are generally young, hip, and cool, often sporting beards and blue jeans.

The first Newman Club was formed back in 1893 by a young medical student at the University of Pennsylvania at Philadelphia, Timothy L. Harrigan. The organization was named after the recently deceased Cardinal John Henry Newman, an English scholar and churchman. Throughout the early 1900s, Newman Clubs were organized at many more institutes of higher education.

In the 1920s and 1930s the Church became increasingly involved with the fledgling Clubs. An outcry arose. Some bishops felt that good Catholics should be educated at Boston College or Holy Cross, not at Columbia or Ohio State. It took a while for the bishops to settle down.

By the early 1960s the Newman Club Federation had joined local clubs into a strong national organization that was formally approved by the American bishops.

Marquette University. Milwaukee, Wisconsin.

In many respects similar to other large Midwestern universities, Marquette reveals its essentially Catholic nature by having great basketball teams and paying no attention at all to football. Many students take their religion quite seriously. A few years back, several protested the showing of the Monty Python film *Life of Brian*.

Gonzaga University. Spokane, Washington.

Lonely outpost of the One True Faith in the overwhelmingly Protestant Northwest, Gonzaga is famous for being the alma mater of Bing Crosby, who later went on to become one of the most famous movie priests of all time in *The Bells of St. Mary's*.

THE GOOD NEWS AND THE BAD NEWS

The Top Catholic Colleges for Basketball and Football

First the good news. There are an astounding number of Catholic colleges that excel in the sport of basketball. An all-time top twenty list follows.* The number of "final four teams" and national championships in this list attests to the superior nature of Catholic B-Ball.

1. Georgetown
2. De Paul (ranked #2 since they can never win the "big one;" they are usually beaten in the first round of the NCAA tourney)
3. Notre Dame
4. University of San Francisco (playing B-Ball again "in the city by the bay")
5. Villanova
6. St. John's (Queens, New York)
7. Marquette
8. Providence
9. Boston College
10. Creighton
11. St. Peter's (Jersey City, New Jersey)
12. Dayton
13. Chaminade (Hawaii's team)
14. Seton Hall (having a tough year)
15. Loyola-Chicago (*the* Loyola for basketball)
16. Fordham
17. Holy Cross
18. St. Bonaventure
19. Iona
20. Duquesne

Touchdown Jesus, Notre Dame

Now the bad news. Possibly due to the huge expenditures required to build a really first-rate football program, Catholic colleges are not terribly deep in this sport. With the exception of the two nationally known biggies, Notre Dame and Boston College, most Catholic colleges reside in Division V.

What follows is a list of the top twenty religious colleges with excellent football.* State universities, the real power in college football, and Ivy League schools, the real joke, have been excluded.

1.	Notre Dame	Catholic
2.	BYU	Mormon
3.	SMU	Methodist
4.	Boston College	Catholic
5.	Texas Christian	Disciples of Christ
6.	Augustana (Illinois)	Lutheran
7.	Wittenberg	Lutheran
8.	Baylor	Baptist
9.	University of Santa Clara	Catholic
10.	Pacific	Church of Christ
11.	Wake Forest	Baptist
12.	Lafayette	Presbyterian
13.	Villanova	Catholic
14.	Furman	Baptist
15.	Richmond	Baptist
16.	Augustana (South Dakota)	Lutheran
17.–20.	Pick 'em	

*Compiled by Steven Davis of Dallas, Texas. Call him, not us.

THE FIRST HOLY COMMUNION CLASS OF 1965

WHERE ARE THEY NOW?

F. X. O'Donnell
Accountant at Big Eight firm.
Total workaholic. Engaged to a
cute paralegal. Doesn't wear
socks with his loafers on weekends. Makes a mean margarita.
Hasn't been to Mass in years.

Patrice Anne Malinowski
Benign dermatologist by day,
writer of horrific medical thrillers
by night. Excelled in biology at
St. Anne's Girls' High. Single,
but looking. Hit-or-miss Mass-
goer.

Mary Elizabeth Barrett
Modern dancer in experimental
dance company in San Francisco. Shares a loft with three
friends. Attends Mass only when
visiting the folks in Boston. Believes that the discipline instilled
in her by the nuns accounts for
her ability to endure the extreme
sacrifice and pain associated
with a career in dance.

John Vincent Minnelli
Semipro football player. Got his
start on the playing fields of Our
Lady Queen of Heaven Parish.
Wears a gold cross on a chain
around his neck. Attends Mass
regularly. Married, has one child
who attends parochial school.

TWO

THE
SALT
OF
THE
EARTH

THE QUINTESSENTIAL CATHOLIC FAMILY

THE QUINTESSENTIAL CATHOLIC MAN

THE QUINTESSENTIAL Catholic man is married. He's tall and handsome, and wears a suit and a hat. The hat is really important. He works for an insurance company, and has a nice wife named Margaret who always wears an apron and has a martini and meat loaf ready for him when he comes home. He walks in the door every night at 5:30, and looks forward to it. Gallivanting around after work not only doesn't appeal to him, it would never *occur* to him. He has four well-scrubbed, very obedient children, the youngest of whom he diapers and puts to bed at night. His station wagon is full of toys, tissues, and coloring books. He has no desire to own a new, black BMW—he couldn't fit the kids or the groceries in it. He likes to barbecue for his family on the weekends, and wears a red-checkered apron that makes his children laugh. He likes going to Mass with his kids on Sundays, and wears a suit and tie because he's an usher. Afterward, so Mom can get some peace and quiet, he takes them to the park or even to meet an ancient nun who taught him math in high school.

The quintessential Catholic man is holy, but in an understated way. He takes his religion seriously, but doesn't make a show of it. The only outward sign of his faith is the Miraculous Medal he wears, or the Rosary on his dresser. You know he believes, though, because he'd never miss Mass and goes to confession regularly.

THE QUINTESSENTIAL CATHOLIC WOMAN

The quintessential Catholic woman's life revolves around the Church. She has numerous children, and spends a good part

The Knights of Columbus

You know them by the ornate hats with the funny-looking plumes, the swords, and the dashing capes. The show-stopping fellows you see at Midnight Mass or marching in the St. Patrick's Day Parade may look pretty silly, but they are part of the world's leading fraternal organization of Catholic men.

The Knights of Columbus were founded in 1882 by Michael J. McGivney, curate of St. Mary's Parish in New Haven, Connecticut. The Knights have members in every state, with approximately 8,400 councils nationwide, and carry out a variety of service programs in addition to holding their renowned dances and potluck dinners.

The inner workings of the K of C are so secret that members swear not to divulge information to anyone, including their families. It is public knowledge, however, that the organization is dedicated to the principles of charity, unity, brotherly love, and patriotism. K of C members can achieve four ranks, each representing a new level of understanding. For initiates, it's worth putting in time, as only the fourth-degree members are allowed to don the impressive regalia.

How to Torture a Catholic Mother

1. Tell her you're not planning to have your baby baptized. Say you'll wait until he's old enough to make up his own mind.
2. Marry a Buddhist in a pagoda.
3. Walk in front of the altar without genuflecting.
4. Throw old palms from Palm Sunday in the trash.
5. Say you think the Mass really has only symbolic meaning, but you go because you like ritual.
6. Wear crucifix earrings like Madonna.
7. If you're a woman, be determined to become a priest.
8. If you're a man, move to San Francisco and dress up in a nun's habit.
9. Call a priest by his first name.
10. Become a priest who people call by his first name.

of her day taking them to school and picking them up again, helping them with their homework, cooking their dinner, doing their laundry, and generally cleaning up after them. But the rest of her time is devoted to the parish.

She volunteers in the playground at lunch and in the school library in the afternoon. After dinner, she goes to meetings of the Mothers' Club or the Rosary-Altar Society. She sells tickets to the parish dances, visits a sick or elderly parishioner, takes Sister to the market, and cleans the altar. Yet she somehow finds time to say the Rosary with her family at least once a week and to slip in an early morning Mass occasionally, all the while keeping track of days of fast and abstinence and Holy Days of Obligation. She is the bedrock on which the parish church is built.

The quintessential Catholic woman has little time or energy for pampering herself. She usually does her own hair and economizes on her wardrobe. She never gets a manicure, though polish adorns her nails sporadically. With her big family, money is often tight, and she has to make a little go a very long way. She is the last person she thinks of or does anything for. The effects of the Me Generation have not filtered down to her, and probably never will.

THE QUINTESSENTIAL CATHOLIC BOY

Sister Mary Perpetua yells out that he's bold and brazen. His mother calls him "all boy." Father Fitzgibbon says he's a smark aleck. We're talking about the quintessential Catholic boy.

In school the quintessential catholic Boy walks a fine line. He knows how to act bad enough to have fun, but not so bad as to get into trouble. He's taught himself to mimic filmstrip beeps, which results in Sister advancing the filmstrip too quickly. When the class is sitting in the dark watching a film like *Photosynthesis and You,* about ten minutes of audio is left when the visual part has finished. Sister is confused. The class is delighted.

On the playground the quintessential Catholic boy hangs out and shoots baskets with the other guys. He's a forward on the Blessed Sacrament team, and would have been a starter this year but the coach is still mad at

him for starting a bonfire in the trash can behind the gym last year.

A couple of days a week the quintessential Catholic boy rides his bike to the nearby grocery store, where he is employed as a "bagger" after school. He puts on his green apron and "Hi, How May I Help You?" button and packs groceries, making sure not to squash the bread with the canned corn.

And, of course, the quintessential Catholic boy is an altar boy. He's conscientious and takes his job seriously, but is not above tucking some incense into his pocket before leaving the sacristy.

Our quintessential Catholic boy is no angel. But despite his mischievousness, he has a pretty good chance of eventually getting to Heaven.

THE QUINTESSENTIAL CATHOLIC GIRL

Virtually every Catholic girl goes through a stage of complete and utter goodness sometime between the ages of eight and twelve. This phase, which lasts anywhere from a few days to several months, is known as the "I want to be a nun" stage. It is at this point that a merely ordinary child is transformed into the quintessential Catholic girl.

She is a model student. When a classmate asks to copy her

homework she says no, but offers to stay with him after school to explain the math equations. When Sister leaves the classroom for a few minutes, the quintessential Catholic girl—because she is the one who seems closest to nunhood—will be asked to watch the class and report any transgressions.

At home the quintessential Catholic girl helps Mom with the dishes, quiets sibling squabbles, and sets the table without being asked. The only time she loses her temper is when her little brother goofs off and refuses to take Mass seriously. In extreme cases, she is known to fast for days at a time, offering up her hunger for the poor souls in Purgatory. Every night before going to sleep she prays fiercely, often for the victims of a natural disaster or for other people she doesn't know.

The slide back to nonquintessential Catholic girlhood behavior often coincides with a blossoming interest in either horses or boys.

THE CATHOLIC HOME

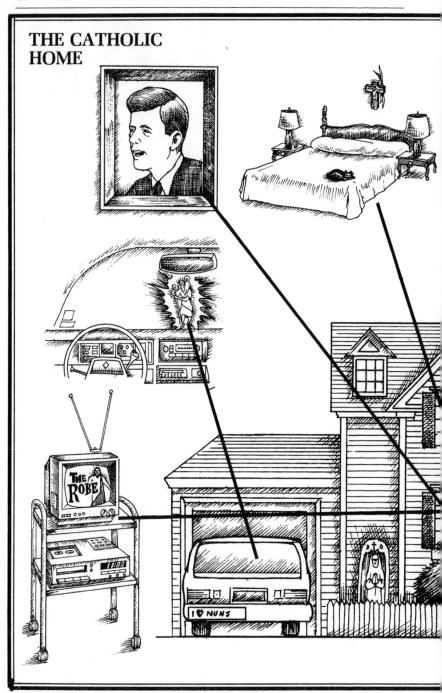

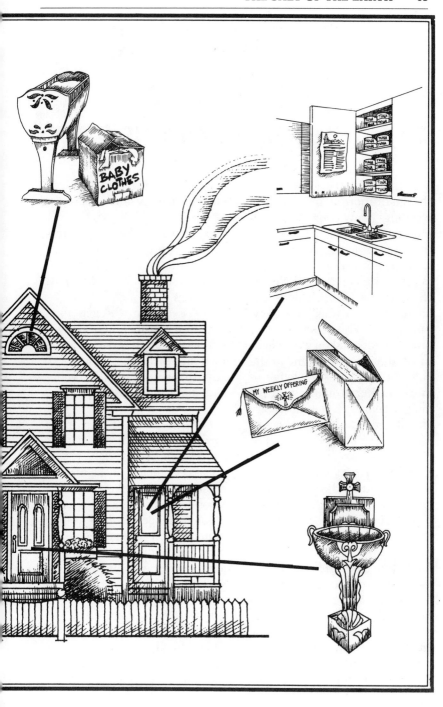

THE CATHOLIC WEDDING

TILL ANNULMENT DO US PART

MUCH MYSTIQUE SURROUNDS the institution of the Catholic wedding. Many consider the requirements rather strict, and so they are, particularly where non-Catholics or previously married persons are concerned. Nevertheless, the Church does not consider itself a wedding factory, and those who wish to have lovely pictures taken at the altar must show commitment to the rules. Test your knowledge of current Church marriage regulations below. (Rules may vary slightly from diocese to diocese.)

The Church does not require that a Catholic marry another Catholic, get married in a Catholic church, or be married by a priest.
True. (Of course, it does strongly encourage all these things.)

The Church requires that a Catholic continue to practice his or her religion, no matter whom he or she marries, and that any children from the marriage be raised in the One True Faith.
True. The part about the children is especially important,

since the whole reason for Catholic marriage is procreation.

Only non-Catholics who marry Catholics are required to sign documents promising that their children will be brought up as Catholics.
False. Everyone who gets married in a Catholic ceremony— even two baptized Catholics marrying each other—must sign such papers. So non-Catholics can stop feeling resentful.

A Catholic may not be married anywhere but in a Catholic church and by a Catholic priest.
False. A Catholic may be married outside of a Catholic church by a non-Catholic minister, but this requires a special dispensation from a bishop. The agreement by both husband and wife to raise any children as Catholics is essential.

Any Catholic can be married by any Catholic priest.
Theoretically true, but in practice often false. Priests are supposed to have evidence that you

are a Catholic in good standing in order to marry you. It helps if you're a member of their parish, and you have to go through pre-marriage counseling or pre-Cana conferences. If you're a member of another parish, what are you trying to hide? Shopping around to find the prettiest church is frowned upon. If you must, do this several years before you plan to be married, and attend Mass regularly.

A Catholic priest may not perform a marriage outside of a Catholic church.
False. This too requires a special arrangement, and, you guessed it, the documents saying the little ones will be loyal to Rome. Marriages conducted by Protestant ministers at which Catholic priests assist are also becoming more and more common.

A Catholic wedding is always a Mass, and therefore interminably long.
False. There is a brief Catholic wedding ceremony that is an alternative to the full Nuptial Mass. It is especially common when a Catholic is marrying a non-Catholic, but it is increasingly used even when two Catholics are getting married. Why? So that everyone can spend more time at the reception consuming watered-down drinks and microwaved food? The church is almost always a more attractice setting than the local motel banquet room, and so it is desirable to remain there for a full hour at least.

YUCKIES (YOUNG URBAN CATHOLICS)

A SPECIAL REPORT

IT'S 11:15 on a Sunday morning, still a tad too early for brunch, outside the lovely old Catholic church in a trendy urban neighborhood. Young people approach the heavy wooden doors and enter in a steady stream. Some come alone, some in couples, some push strollers containing fat-cheeked little cherubs. Attire ranges from Weekend Cazh to Almost Nice Enough for a Job Interview, but you can tell that just about everyone is wearing designer labels. Little alligators even peek out from inside the

Apricas. The only thing missing is a hitching post for Akitas.

But wait a minute. Aren't young people supposed to be staying away from the Church in droves? Is this just a bishop's daydream? What's going on here?

Contrary to what you might expect, the antinuclear movement has not rented out the church for a weekend meeting. This is not a CYO *Big Chill* reunion. The church is not raffling off VCRs. And the people going into the church are not the garden-variety Yuppies they appear to be, but Yuckies (Young Urban Catholics). Are they as bad as the name sounds? Let's take a closer look.

The word on the young Catholic grapevine is that Yuckies are indeed going back to church. The stream has not yet turned into a flood, but the holy water is rising to serve an increasing number of manicured fingers. At parties, one hears things like, "My girlfriend is a Catholic. I mean a real Catholic—someone who goes to church every week." Anecdotes start off with, "When

---

Are You a Catholic? A Quiz to Make Sure

1. Which of these does not belong with the others?
   A. Holy, Holy, Holy
   B. Holy Orders
   C. Holy Spirit
   D. Holy Cow
2. Going to Mass on nine consecutive First Fridays signifies that
   A. you are very holy and Sister Clothilde would be proud of you.
   B. TGIF takes on a new meaning.
   C. you are guaranteed to have a priest with you when you die.
3. You are willing to die for your faith
   A. by being thrown into a lion's den and eaten alive.
   B. in a freak hunting accident.
4. Eight years in a parochial school guarantees that
   A. you have a healthier-than-normal respect for authority.
   B. there is a 99-to-1 chance that you can still say the Act of Contrition by heart.
   C. you understand the concept of a clean milk bottle.
   D. all of the above.
5. May 13, 1917, was the date
   A. Our Lady first visited Fatima.
   B. beanie first worn by a parochial school girl in America.

I was at Mass last week . . ." Strangely, this reminds you of the party your mother had after your little nephew got baptized, the one all your aunts and uncles came to.

To be sure, some Yuckies are still closet cases. Like the early Christians, they keep their faith a secret and know each other only by special signs. They wake up before dawn, sneak off to the 6:15 A.M. Mass, and return before their housemates have awoken. Others, when asked where they go every Sunday morning, say they are having an affair with a married person or give some other socially acceptable explanation.

Still other Yuckies are thought to arrive at early Mass directly from nightclubs. Spiky hair, sunglasses, and studded leather are reportedly no longer unusual sights at daybreak services. And how else to explain the limos and cabs blocking the church gates?

But why have the Yuckies returned to Mass? Have they really gotten religion? Is it just that they're getting older? Or is it that they feel comfortable in a place where black has always been a chic color? Perhaps it's a bit of all of these. Whether the trend will last is hard to say. But it's certainly one that will be watched with great interest by Church leaders.

YOU CAN'T GO HOME AGAIN . . . OR CAN YOU?

REASONS TO REJOIN THE CHURCH

MAYBE YOU WERE AWAY for a long time, and maybe there were some pretty serious disagreements. Now you want to patch things up again. Just remember that the Church has changed, too, and that things won't be exactly the same as when you left. Try not to be too upset about this. Isn't that why you left in the first place—because things never changed? Here are a host of honorable and merely convenient reasons to come back into the fold.

1. It's respectable to have a religion again.
Do-you-own-thingism is definitely over, even in the spiritual realm. You want something solid, something with tradition, something hard-boiled. Something that looks substantial on college applications, army dog tags, and hospital admittance forms. You want a religion that says, "We treat sinners the old-fashioned way—we burn 'em!" For those on the rise in business and politics, nothing bespeaks wholesomeness and dependability of character like church membership. Caution: If you are looking for respectability only, become an Episcopalian.

2. If you must continue to dissent, there's a lot more tolerance than there used to be.
In fact, it's very hard these days to get thrown out for being a freethinker, since the clergy and religious tend to be much more liberal than the laity. Let's just not go over the top like the Dutch and start throwing things at the Pope.

3. It's a great excuse for leaving boring Saturday night parties early.
Even if you later decide to throw a movie on the VCR or go out dancing at an all-night club, you can still catch the 5:30 Mass on Sunday afternoon.

4. As a regular Mass-goer, you'll be more welcome at the big holiday services everyone and his brother wants to attend.

5. If you're a diehard fan of the Latin Mass, you can probably search out a parish offering an approved version of the ancient rite.
Just don't be surprised when your references to any post-1965 phenomena—such as Watergate, the space shuttle, or "Wheel of Fortune"—are met with a blank stare from fellow parishioners.

6. The priests give better sermons.
They've got to draw crowds these days, like the poor Protestant ministers always had to do to keep their jobs.

7. To get married.
If it's just to please your parents, it doesn't count.

8. To get your baby baptized.
This always counts. Even if you choose not to save your own soul

from going to Hell, you've saved baby's soul from going wherever it would go now that it no longer goes to limbo.

9. You're very unlikely to happen upon a Guitar Mass these days.
Tradition is back in music, too. If you're really lucky you'll get a well-drilled choir singing motets or Gregorian chant. At worst, you'll have to endure "Pachelbel's Canon" on the organ.

10. The Sacrament of Reconciliation.
It used to be called Confession. You don't have to recite every little peccadillo to the priest anymore in order to have your sins absolved. It's done en masse, for you and the rest of the congregation. If this is a little too generic for your taste, individual consultation is still available upon request.

11. The Second Coming might be coming sooner than you think.
Still the biggest and best reason of all. "As it was in the beginning, is now and ever shall be . . . " Amen.

ALL IN THE FAMILY
ETHNIC CATHOLICS

SPELLED WITH A SMALL "c," the word "catholic" means universal, comprehensive, and broad-minded. The Church has always been composed of diverse nationalities and ethnic groups. These groups have not always been celebrated for their broad-mindedness, however, toward non-Catholics or even toward each other. The chief characteristics of some of the major Catholic divisions, at least as seen by *other* Catholics, are as follows.

IRISH
The Irish have a peculiarly humorless approach to religion, except at wakes and funerals. For this reason and others, they are thought to be puritanical and hypocritical. If the Italians control the international organization, the Irish have a near-monopoly on the U.S. franchise. St. Patrick's Day—with its green beer, drunken paraders, and "Kiss Me, I'm Irish" buttons—is perhaps the most festive feast day of the entire liturgical calendar.

ITALIANS

Extremely lax in Mass attendance, except for grandmothers dressed in black from head to toe and children under ten years of age. Inclined to adulation of obscure saints, in whose honor they regularly hold gaudy, paganistic festivals. Still, they have maintained a fierce grip on the Vatican hierarchy.

ANGLO-CATHOLICS

All right, they're not really Catholics—they waffle on allegiance to the Pope. But otherwise they've got the best of both worlds—British manners combined with Catholic spirituality. Writers no less distinguished than T. S. Eliot eloquently argue their case. Unless the Anglican and Catholic churches are reunited, these people will continue to occupy a very special niche.

EASTERN EUROPEANS

Collectively, these groups are noted for their dislike of one another. Lithuanians dislike Estonians, Estonians dislike Czechs, Czechs dislike Poles, Poles dislike Ukrainians, Slovenians dislike Bohemians, and so on. Irish priests were known to say that going to the Polish church didn't count because you couldn't understand what they where saying. Lord knows how they justified the Latin Mass all those years. The Poles have got the Pope now, though, and Eastern European weddings are great.

HISPANICS

Very devout, very mystical, very obedient. How else would they have such huge families? And what baseball fan can forget Jesus Alou reverently blessing himself before stepping into the

batter's box? In Latin America, however, the clergy shows a decidely unpassive approach to social change. Both there and here, Mother Church is losing a percentage of her faithful Latin flock to (God forbid!) Protestant evangelicals. A sharp increase in boisterous Hispanic charismatic services in Catholic churches has been noted.

FRANCO-AMERICANS

The Franco-Americans are right up there with the Irish for strict observance, which perhaps accounts for the intense former rivalry between French and Irish clergy in New England, Louisiana, and Canada. In these parts of North America, everyone learns to call a nativity scene a *crèche*. The Franco-Americans, as one might expect, bring a definite *savoir faire* to their wonderful cuisine, and their traditional Christmas suppers after *messe de minuit* (Midnight Mass) are well worth brushing up on your high school French for.

Who will be the next Catholic U.S. President?

Ted
Kennedy

Mario
Cuomo

Geraldine
Ferraro

Bruce
Springsteen

BLACKS

God bless their souls. After all those years of Protestant indoctrination in the South, they've still managed to find the One True Church. There aren't very many yet, but surely their numbers will grow as more urban black children attend Catholic schools because there's discipline and the education is better. African Catholics are really testing the Pope's patience, though, saying that clerical celibacy isn't part of their tradition.

UPON THIS ROCK 'N' ROLL

POP STARS WHO GREW UP CATHOLIC

Madonna. Her Crucifix earrings, her Rosary necklaces, even her name may annoy some traditionalists, but Madonna comes by her Catholic iconography honestly. From an early age, she rebelled against her strict upbringing. At school, she put bright panty bloomers on underneath her drab uniform and hung upside down from the monkey bars. She and a friend once peeked through the windows of a convent to see nuns without their habits on, confirming a suspicion that the Sisters indeed had hair. Nevertheless, Madonna confesses that as a child she thought nuns were beautiful. For a time she even wanted to be one, proving beyond a shadow of a doubt that she is essentially a good Catholic girl.

Cyndi Lauper. Cyndi holds the distinction of being thrown out of two Catholic schools—the first a neighborhood parochial school in New York City ("because my mother was divorced"), the second a convent boarding school in upstate New York. Her nun stories make most people's pale by comparison. "One time I scratched this girl's back," Cyndi remembers. "A nun ran in, beat me, and called me a lesbian. I didn't know what a lesbian was." Fortunately, Cyndi survived her Catholic school experiences intact. Her clothes, like Madonna's, are about as far from the dull uniformity of Catholic school garb as you can get.

Bob Geldof. Already dubbed "Saint Bob," Band Aid/Live Aid organizer Geldof has not always had the most cordial of relationships with Mother Church. Sent as a young boy to a Catholic school near Dublin run by the Holy Ghost Fathers, Geldof incurred their wrath when he replaced his classmates' catechisms with copies of Chairman Mao's *Little Red Book*. He later committed an even more heinous offense when he refused to wear the school blazer, and for his pains was branded an "insidious influence" by the Good Fathers. Despite such inauspicious beginnings, Geldof's informal beatification ultimately may prove to be not far from the mark. A Nobel Peace Prize nominee, Geldof is responsible for raising more than $130 million worldwide to combat famine. He has literally saved millions of people from certain death. If that doesn't qualify as a modern-day miracle, what does?

Bruce Springsteen. Bruce began his rock'n'roll career in his hometown of Freehold, New Jersey, in a high-school band called the Castiles. The Castiles often played CYO dances and were regulars at a Freehold teen club called the Left Foot, which was started by a Catholic priest named Father Coleman. Like many other teen clubs and "drop-in centers" started by Catholic priests in the late 1960s, the Left Foot featured music, low-key social activities, and nonalcoholic drinks. Though Bruce doesn't talk much about his Catholic upbringing, his compassion and concern for others are eloquent testimony to his character. If he weren't already Catholic, we'd certainly wish that he was.

Famous Catholics

Babe Ruth	Al Pacino
Vince Lombardi	Robert De Niro
Roger Maris	Frank Zappa
Brooke Shields	Lech Walesa
Sean Penn	Christa McAuliffe
Jesus Alou	Alexander Haig
Matty Alou	Pierre Trudeau
Felipe Alou	Brian Mulroney
Phil Simms	Declan McManus
Bianca Jagger	Corazon Aquino
Mick Jagger	James Cagney

The Holy Name Society

Frank Church
Joey Bishop
Dr. Joyce Brothers
Judas Priest
James Deacon
Lance Parrish
Patricia Neal
Alexander Pope
Dave Concepcion
Cardinal Sin (*no kidding*)

ST. ROSE OF LIMA BY ANY OTHER NAME:
Least Popular Parish Names

Virtually every Catholic has at one time or another attended Mass at a Sacred Heart or a St. Mary's. How many, however, can boast of having set foot inside a St. Florian's or a St. Gall's? Parish names, like children's names, go in and out of vogue. Those with the less-attractive names are more likely to suffer from inferiority complexes. So the next time you meet someone from one of the following parishes—whose names are not exactly at the height of fashion—be charitable.

St. Adalbert's	St. Finbar's	St. Kilian's
St. Aloysius	St. Florian's	St. Leonard's
St. Alphonsus	St. Gall's	St. Mel's
St. Benedict the Moor	St. Hedwig's	St. Rita's
St. Casimir's	St. John Kanty	St. Sylvester's
SS. Cyril and Methodius	St. John of Nepomuk	The Gesu
St. Emeric's	St. Josaphat's	

FOOD, GLORIOUS FOOD

MAN MAY NOT LIVE by bread alone, but breaking bread together is an indispensable part of life as a Catholic. From the sticky glazed doughnuts at the post-Mass coffee hour to the dried-out macaroni and cheese in the school cafeteria, sustenance is all important. These communal eats nourish both body and soul.

THE BAKE SALE

Items offered: Brownies
M&M cookies (ever popular)
Pound cake (never popular)
Rice Krispies squares
Drooping meringue pies
Cupcakes with red-hot candy decorations
"Bundt" cakes

Comments: Usually a fund-raiser for something like a CYO
field trip. Note that the recipients of the funds
do not bake. Not only does the mother throw together something at the last minute ("Mom, I
need a cake by tomorrow"), but she must also
purchase a neighbor's equally haphazard crea-
tion. At the sale everything looks misshapen,
melting, lumpy, or evil. Little cards naming items
like "Sponge Cake Delight" are helpful in iden-
tifying culinary inventions that are perplexing at
first glance.

THE COFFEE HOUR

Always served: Coffee from big urns
Lipton tea and hot water
Cremora, sugar cubes, Sweet 'N' Low
Popsicle stick stirrers, Styrofoam cups, paper
napkins
Glazed doughnuts

Comments: Usually held after Mass in the church basement.
Always purposeful—come meet the exotic missionary, the new pastor, etc. Lots of cigarette
smoke, folding chairs, fidgety children. Adult
conversation on civic affairs and other boring
topics reaches a dull roar. To be avoided at all
costs.

THE PANCAKE BREAKFAST

Menu: Plain or blueberry pancakes with maple syrup
                 Orange juice
                 Coffee, tea, milk for children

Comments: Smiling Dads serve heaps of flapjacks and urge
                 extra helpings on the unsuspecting. Copious
                 jokes on "Dad's cooking." Takes place in the
                 school cafeteria, replete with folding chairs, paper
                 tablecloths. Later in the day, children complain
                 of stomachaches.

THE SCHOOL CAFETERIA

The week's menus: Monday—Baked ravioli
                    Tuesday—Grilled-cheese sandwiches
                    Wednesday—Beans 'n' franks
                    Thursday—Hamburgers
                    Friday—Fish sticks
                    Assorted vegetables: lima beans, instant
                    mashed potatoes, cubed carrots 'n' peas, green
                    Jell-O with dab of mayo on top
                    Best dessert: ice cream sandwich
                    Worst dessert: fruit
                    Most common dessert: tapioca, apple brown
                    betty (tie)

Comments: *Loud*. Odor of milk cartons, peanut butter,
                    overripe fruit. Nun patrol. Some kids bring
                    sack lunches, trade fruit with tablemates.
                    Grossest memory: dead fly in chicken pie.

THE NEW YEAR'S EVE PARISH DANCE

Offerings: Open bar with cut-rate liquors
                    Plentiful Chex party mix

Comments: Held in the parish gym, basketball hoops pulled
                    up. Festive crepe paper and balloon decorations.
                    Everyone drinks from plastic champagne glasses
                    with detachable stems. Band arranged for by the
                    president of the parish council's brother-in-law.
                    "Fast" dances baffle husbands, aerobicized wives
                    rock out. Priests loiter agreeably around the en-
                    trance. Bartenders are the same guys who vol-
                    unteer to be ushers every Sunday.

THE POST-CHRISTENING PARTY

Often served: Chips with Lipton onion dip
                    Sliced turkey, ham, roast beef, bread, rolls, mus-
                    tard, mayo
                    Casseroles: tuna, scalloped potatoes, American
                    chop suey
                    Molded salads
                    Layer cakes and pies
                    Liquor
                    Cake from the bakery is always white and has
                    the baby's name written on it in either pink or
                    blue frosting.

Comments: Discussion centers around the degree to which
                    baby did or didn't cry in church.

KNIGHTS OF COLUMBUS BUFFET

Help yourself to: Salads—carrot and raisin, three-bean, tossed
                    iceberg
                    Sandwiches—egg salad and tuna salad, with
                    crusts cut off
                    Baked beans, slaw, potato salad
                    Crockpot fare   Lasagna
                    Fried chicken   Sheet cakes

Comments: Hurricane lamps and Italian-tavern checkered
                    tablecloths adorn the K of C hall. Polka tunes on
                    static-ridden sound system. Priest gives blessing,
                    then honors a table by joining it.

PARISH LAY EMPLOYEES

While it's the nuns and priests we always hear about, there are a host of peripheral attendants in every parish whose contributions aren't as obvious.

Rectory Housekeeper

A goodly soul, devoted to the priests. Is either a very good or a very bad cook. Dons a freshly ironed apron daily. Favorite saying: "Have you eaten?"

School Janitor

A hard worker, but duties are generally few, as the nuns instruct children to keep classrooms and playground scrupulously tidy.

Parish Gardener

A whiz at clipping topiary in the shape of saints, and his green thumb is legendary. Parish ladies ask him for advice on mealybugs and drooping African violets.

Lay Teachers

The ultimate in unsung heroes. They do the same job as the nuns, but without the benefit of a habit, and have to work harder for respect.

Cafeteria Ladies

Generous moms who donate their time flipping burgers and cubing Jell-O. They learn how to dispense everything from succotash to turkey stuffing with an ice cream scoop.

The Choir

The benefits of being in the choir are a guaranteed seat and a panaramic view of Mass proceedings. It is unfortunate that anyone who likes to sing is welcome to join most parish choirs.

The Organist

Consistently plays one beat slower than the choir is singing.

Ushers

Time-pressed parish men figure that since they're at Mass every Sunday anyway, they might as well take up the collection and gain a little grace in the process.

Counters

Some ushers stay after Mass to count the bills and roll the coins. For the truly dedicated only.

Dear Abbey,

I know that from time to time you answer questions on the various changes that have occurred in our Church since Vatican II. Well, I have never heard a decent explanation from priests, nuns, or ushers of certain changes that I find very disturbing. For instance, why does everyone go around calling the Holy Ghost the Holy Spirit? I mean, when we used to go to church as children we were inspired with awe at the intonations of Latin, the indirect lighting, and the smells of rare incense that wafted through our services. If someone said something about the Holy Ghost, well, that would send chills up and down your spine. Where's the mystery now? Where's the romance?

—Mrs. Fud D. Duddey

Dear Mrs. Duddey,

Your is a good question, unlike many that I have to read through and answer. So I am going to give it to you straight. The Holy Ghost is now the Holy Spirit for one simple reason: He scared

people. Remember that Hitchcock film *The Birds*? Well, after that everybody was looking over his shoulder every time the Holy Ghost was mentioned. Not only was He a "bird," but He was a "ghost" to boot. The Church Fathers decided they just couldn't have one of the Trinity going around scaring the bejabbers out of people. Yes, I agree it added a little more mystery and romance to things, but the Church wisely decided that going to church should not be like going to see *Halloween III*.

Dear Abbey,

Our church has recently begun having trouble with people coming to Mass late. The blacktopping of the new parking lots has forced many to park far away and consequently people come in after the priest has already begun to celebrate Mass. It is very disturbing for us who had enough common sense to come a little bit earlier on days when the parking lots are going to be blacktopped. Help us return to our services the quiet and dignity that they deserve. **—Ticked at the Tardy**

Dear Ticked,

I myself have been rudely disturbed by the late arrival of those who have not had the foresight or courtesy to arrive on time. My church has recently begun printing a message on the Offertory Envelopes that one of our council members said worked quite well at Broadway theaters: "Latecomers will be seated at the discretion of the management!"

Dear Abbey,

We still hear and read lots of stuff about Vatican II in the news. I thought that was over ages ago. Can it really still be going on? Also, I don't ever remember hearing about Vatican I. Did I miss it?

—**Squeamish About Sequels**

Dear Squeamish,

You really have got me stumped on this one. I don't remember a Vatican I either, unless it was just called Vatican, like the films after *Rocky* were called II, III, and IV, but the first one was just *Rocky*. The Vatican II meeting is not itself going on, but as they like to say at the Vatican, "the work of Vatican II" is.

Dear Abbey,

I have noticed that the younger priests at our parish rarely wear their Roman collars outside of church. Even some of the older priests are showing up at the shopping mall in Ralph Lauren shirts. What is the origin of the Roman collar and why aren't priests wearing them outside of church anymore?

—**A Concerned Clotheshorse**

Dear Clotheshorse,

I hope you will understand that Dear Abbey generally doesn't answer questions on fashion since her true calling is to instruct the faithful on matters of manners and faith. This disturbing trend, however, may well be a matter of good manners on the part of the priests. The nice thing about priests wearing Roman collars outside of church was that the faithful could easily identify them at the grocery store or on the golf course and not let slip with some blasphemy or bad language. The trend toward casual wear for priests, which has made the Roman collar all but obsolete, may however be turning around. The fashion trend started on the television program "Miami Vice" has returned Italian fashion to the cutting edge of couture. Some of the older Italian designers, like the ones who developed the Roman collar, may be able to ride this fashion wave and return the collar to its former place of prominence among priests. In answer to your question about the origin of the Roman collar, I have no idea.

Dear Abbey,

I am a good Catholic. I was shocked the other day to hear a nun on television say she saw no reason why she couldn't be a priest. What is wrong with nuns today?! I think it all has to do with rock music and the way people dress today. Look at Michael Jackson and Prince and David Bowie. Boys look like girls, girls look like boys, and now nuns want to be priests. What's going on?

—**Not a Michael Jackson fan**

Dear Not,

Dear Abbey hates questions she can't answer, but not that much. You obviously have not "come a long way, baby," but so be it. If you care to pen a song called "Girls Just Wanna Be Nuns," that's your business. But Dear Abbey doesn't have to listen.

Dear Abbey,

What is the world coming to? I heard that on one of the Pope's trips (I like to follow the Pope's trips around the world on my wall map, with colored pushpins marking his journeys) a bishop in Holland, or maybe it was Luxembourg or somewhere close to France, was rude to the Holy Father. How dare they!? What can be done with those who are rude to our Pope?

—**A Pope Watcher**

Dear Watcher,

Your concern for the feelings of the Pontiff are truly Christian and I am sure he would be touched by your concern, but let me set your mind at rest: The Pope can handle himself. I also am a closet "Pope watcher" and hang on every word of the news reports about his travels. But the Holy Father has developed a bag of tricks to disarm those who do not have sufficient respect for his Holy Office. You know that little smile he always has on his face? Can you imagine too many people saying anything really nasty to him while he's smiling his little smile? And have you noticed how sometimes when someone is rude to the Pope he will put his face in his hands for a second and then the person who said the nasty thing will be embarrassed and feel bad and then the Pope will smile his little smile and bless them as if to say, "You're a jerk, but no hard feelings." So, although your concern is touching, rest assured he didn't get to be the Pope by being a wimp.

Dear Abbey,

I am occasionally a lector for our church. I consider it a great honor to assist the priest in the reading of the Scriptures, and it also gives me an opportunity to use my stage voice, which landed me the lead in many school plays. Recently, however, I have noticed an increase in chuckling and smirking on the part of the congregation when I infrequently mispronounce the name of an archaic saint or Bible figure, or when I clear my throat. I think someone should address the problem of the congregation's rudeness to those who are willing to take on the responsibility of being a lector, before we all quit in disgust.

—**Developing Stage Fright**

Dear Fright,

I'm afraid you are not going to get much sympathy from Dear Abbey on this one. I have found myself snickering on occasion at the bungling of a lector who has just realized he has been speaking for ten minutes with the mike off. The increasing use of nonprofessional lectors, also sometimes called commentators, has been a serious problem in many churches since the practice became widespread in the 1970s. I think the problem could be solved by adopting a few simple rules:

1. No children should ever be allowed to read at any sort of Mass. They are too short to reach the mike on the lectern,

2. Relatives of the priest should not be allowed to read, even if they are in town from Topeka just for that day.

3. Before becoming a lector, one should receive some instruction on how to behave at the lectern. There is altogether too much frenzied gripping of the lectern, tapping of the microphone, and coughing out of the side of the mouth. There are some very good books on public speaking by some of our finest practitioners of the art. I would suggest recent tomes by Jack Valenti or Steve Allen.

Dear Abbey,

After Mass recently, I confronted Father Bob about what I feel to be a growing problem at our services. Whenever the time comes for the faithful to return to their seats after Communion, the sound of the kneelers hitting the floor shakes the church like the Guns of Navarone booming in the distance. He claims he doesn't hear it, but when I am meditating after Communion the noise shocks me out of my sacred bliss. What do you think can be done to stop this disturbing noise?   —**Shell-Shocked**

Dear Shocked,

Frankly, I think the designers of the standard kneeler must have had a little bit of the Devil in them if the high incidence of bruised shins, crushed toes, and sonic booms caused by the lowering and raising of these knee-savers is any indication. But Dear Abbey does have a solution. Remember all those felt-appliqué banners the church used to hang all over the place? Just cut them up and apply them to the underside of the kneelers. You will not only reduce the noise level in the church but rid it of eyesores as well.

THREE

POVERTY, CHASTITY, AND OBEDIENCE

ANY COLOR AS LONG AS IT'S BLACK

NUNS AND PRIESTS were the ones who got the calling at some point in their young lives, like everyone else. Unlike everyone else, they found that the calling was more than a passing fancy.

Priests and nuns train long and hard to perfect their vocation and to prepare for religious service. There is a long period of years during which they are perfectly free to say "Thanks but no thanks," and return to the secular world with no hard feelings.

Nuns in the earliest stages are known as postulants. They become novices after a while, and eventually, if all goes smoothly, take their final vows. Final vows, for a nun, are as important as a wedding vow. At the ceremony, nuns go so far as to don white gowns and gold rings, entitling them to be called "Brides of Christ."

The ordination of a priest is an equally impressive affair. Priests spend years as seminarians before receiving the sacrament, called Holy Orders, which gives them their special powers. During one point in the ordination ceremony, they are required to prostrate themselves on the floor in front of the Bishop, as a symbol of their obedience to his will.

Obedience is one of the chief hallmarks of the religious life, the other two being poverty and chastity. Why anyone would embrace such conditions of life in this day and age is a mystery to many, including the great majority of young people. Vocations to the religious life have been declining for years, but there is no indication that the requirements will be made any easier. Like the Marines—tough and proud of it—the Church is looking for a few good men, and women.

HOLY ORDERS
OUR FAVORITE FELLOWS

THE CHRISTIAN BROTHERS

The Christian Brothers are renowned for making wine and brandy, and for teaching. For many years they wore stiff white cloth tablets (without the Ten Commandments actually written on them) under their chins. They are known as strict disciplinarians, and the chafing of their tablets under their chins explains their resulting short-temperedness. They are not afraid to use their fists in a dangerous classroom situation, such as when a student forgets his homework.

THE JESUITS

Known as the thinkers and intellectuals of the priesthood, they are so different from other priests that their leader is known as the "Black Pope." This does not refer either to his skin color or his character, but to the fact that he has an extraordinary degree of power and dresses in black, rather than the splendid colors in which the Pope is usually decked out. Founded by nobleman-soldier-poet-cavalier St. Ignatius Loyola, the Jesuits never shy away from wordly challenges and were often the first Catholic missionaries on the scene in newly discovered territories. The evil Portuguese priest in *Shogun,* for example, was a Jesuit. The Jesuits have gained a reputation for maintaining the highest standards of scholarship in their schools and universities, which include Georgetown, Holy Cross, Marquette, Boston College, and, naturally, all those Loyolas. The Jesuits are particularly proud of their Father Marquette (discovered the Mississippi) and Father Isaac Jogues (martyred by Mohawk Indians).

ST. VINCENT DE PAUL AND THE CHARITABLE ORDERS

St. Vincent de Paul founded the Society that bears his name. He led a very exciting life. As a boy he hollowed out a tree trunk, made it into a chapel, and spent much time there. Later captured by Turks in corsairs, he was sold as a slave to a fisherman, but as he was no sailor, he was resold to an alchemist. He was resold once again, and ran away with his master to Europe, where his master joined the Do-Good Brothers. Many other terrible things happened to St. Vincent de Paul, including being falsely accused of stealing a large sum of money, but through it all he remained a charitable man. He died broke.

THE DOMINICANS

The Dominicans are a particularly fascinating order because of the number of names they have been called. The "Order of Preachers" was founded by St. Dominic in 1216. The Dominicans were soon being called "Domini Canes," or "Dogs of the Lord," because of the speed with which the order spread. In England they are called "Blackfriars" because of their black habits, and in France they are known as "Jacobins" since their headquarters was on Rue St. Jacques.

THE BENEDICTINES

St. Benedict is best known for civilizing barbarians, especially Goths. The Benedictines produce a great liqueur, also called Benedictine, while helps make after-dinner drinks a civilizing experience.

NECTARS OF GOD
RELIGIOUS LIQUEURS

FOR CENTURIES, monks have supported themselves by making after-dinner drinks. Indeed, there is considerable evidence that monks actually invented the making of liqueurs. Often located in the beautiful backwaters of Europe, their monasteries were ravaged time and again by pagan marauders, plague, and religious wars. They needed an absolutely dependable, secure trade, and what could be more dependable than liquor? Especially when it was made from a unique combination of local herbs, plants, and fruits; it took years and years to make; and the formula was as closely guarded as the recipe for Kentucky Fried Chicken. The following varieties of earthly ambrosia are among the oldest and most famous of the monastical products.

BENEDICTINE

First produced in 1510, Benedictine is thought to be the

world's oldest liqueur. The complex process of making it, involving almost thirty ingredients, takes three years. After that, the drink must be aged for four more years before it is ready to imbibe. Benedictine originated at an abbey in Normandy, and was made there continuously until the place was pillaged during the French Revolution. Fortunately, the formula was not lost, and commercial production began in 1863.

CHARTREUSE

Still produced by the same order of Carthusian monks that invented it in the sixteenth century, Chartreuse is perhaps the most subtle and intriguing of all the herbal liqueurs. Its yellow-green hues are so distinctive that its name has come to describe a range of colors as well as a drink.

Despite appearances, the concoction is all natural, containing the essences of more than 130 herbs and spices and taking flavor from the oak casks in which it is aged. Visitors to France can drop in at the distillery near Grenoble. Only three monks, sworn to vows of silence, know the formula.

VIEILLE CURÉ

The religious origins of this French liqueur are betrayed by its very name, which means "old priest." Based on a mixture of cognac and Armagnac, Vieille Curé incorporates the flavors of some fifty herbs and is produced at the Abbey of Cedon in Bordeaux. Like Chartreuse, it comes in shades of yellow and green. If the name is not enough to convey spiritual associations, the "stained glass" packaging is sure to get the message across.

PRIESTS WE HAVE KNOWN

IN THE LATE 1960s the media made much of priests who were leaving their orders to enter the secular world. This left many Catholics wondering who would be left to run the parish. Never fear. The great "silent majority" of priests, many of whom never entertained notions of leaving, have been on duty tending their flocks. The following are among the most colorful and best-loved.

FATHER HOLE-IN-ONE

"Being a Catholic is like learning to play the game of golf. It's something you can do for a lifetime and never get right. Oh, but the hope of a hole-in-one or a perfectly executed sandblast keeps us going." So begins a typical sermon by Father Hole-in-One. Long the pastor of St. Burning Tree by the Water, he looks forward to Sundays as his day to wrest the clubs from his bag after celebrating 12:30 Mass. In an imperfect world, Father finds a few perfect hours on the links with his new set of Ben Hogans and his Top-Flites. He feels communing with nature and his six-iron brings him closer to HIM. Father's language on the course, however, can be spicy. "Mother Mary," he shouts as an errant drive strikes a tree.

"Oh, take a Mulligan," his trusty golfing partner, the Bishop, chortles. "Saints be praised," Father Hole-in-One gasps, after negotiating a tricky downhill putt for his double-bogie. "Christ!" he screams as the foursome behind them drives a ball right over their heads. "Father, forgive them," the Bishop snickers, rising to his feet. "They know not what they do!"

FATHER HAVE-A-NIP

Jolly, red-faced Father Have-a-Nip is a saintly man who forever seems to have a small smile glued to his countenance. Never known to be fond of the early Masses, he does, however, have an excellent relationship with the congregation. Rather than try to hash out all the parish problems on the front steps of the church, Father has an open-door policy at the rectory, where his equally saintly housekeeper, Mrs. Rottenelli, keeps his study amply stocked with refreshments. Father is not against any member of the parish coming over after Mass to have a few belts and to unburden his heart. Father also knows that good Irish or Scotch whiskey is a great tongue loosener for the troubled in his care. He is partial to any of the Johnnie Walkers, but is only really in Heaven when one of the faithful sends him a bottle

of Glenlivet at Christmas. While having a nightcap or two, Father has been known to captivate family gatherings for hours with his stories of traveling across the country by train with the Archbishop.

FATHER FIRE-AND-BRIMSTONE

Many members of Father's small parish in Kansas think the Good Father was dropped on his head as a child. For what else could account for his graphic descriptions of the tortures of Hell? The way Father talks at Mass, you would think he had already been there. Some of the more wry among his parishioners have taken to numbering his sermons. "The Omen III, the Last Gospel" was one of their favorites. It began with Father giving a suitable Lenten address and then quickly admonishing the group to imagine the worst possible thing they could. Children contemplated no candy for a month, and adulterers imagined discovery. Father just stood at the pulpit tapping his toe and smirking. After five minutes of silence, he asked quietly, "Are you all imagining the worst thing that could happen to you?" The congregation nodded. "Well," Father fairly screeched into the microphone, "that's what Hell is like! Years and years and eons and eons of the worst possible thing you could imagine. Centuries and millenniums! Constant, everlasting, continuing, without end! The worst thing you could imagine! I hope I have made my point."

FATHER STRUM-A-TUNE

In the sleepy parish of the Church of Holy Civil Disobedience, not far from the campus of the University of California at Berkeley, resides a throwback to those halcyon days of protest

marches and felt-appliqué vestments. He is Father Strum-a-Tune, and he remembers the 1960s as a time when right was right, wrong was wrong, and priests were as likely to be marching with Dr. King as scribbling soon-forgotten sermons in the rectory. In fact, Father Strum-a-Tune joined the priesthood in order to bring a new social conscience to the flock.

Among Father's many accom-

Be All That You Can Be: The Church Hierarchy

The Priest. He is the foot soldier in the Army of Christ, roughly equivalent to the private in the regular army. His job is to administer the sacraments to the Faithful. Directly responsible to everyone in the hierarchy above him. Some priests make very good novelists, rabblerousers or, formerly, congressmen.

The Monsignor. The Staff Sergeant of the Church, his frock is festooned with red piping and red buttons. When schoolchildren see the Monsignor in his red and black garb, they are instantly impressed.

The Bishop. The Lieutenant of the Church, he is in charge of many parishes and priestly foot soldiers. The Bishop is the official governor of the diocese and is empowered to make laws, as long as they are not in conflict with Church Law. Has many of the trappings of the Pope: brocade vestments and big ring.

The Archbishop. The Major of the Church, he is usually a bishop with a large diocese (appropriately called an archdiocese) and usually has a shot at being made cardinal. He has good access to the Pope and can always rat on someone who isn't doing what he wants them to do.

The Cardinal. He is a General of the Church, and usually has a television show in his hometown. Like a senator of the United States, the Cardinal is a member of an extremely exclusive club. His garb is royal red. Get to know him well, since he could be your next Pope.

The Pope. The Commander in Chief. *Numero Uno. Il Papa.* He is the head of the Church on earth, and what he says goes. Wonderful perks go along with the job, like living in Vatican City and having a really terrific white wardrobe. But he has responsibilities that would drive a lesser man to drink the sacramental serving wine.

plishments—which often landed him in the pages of national news magazines—were the "Jazz Mass" for folk guitar, the national best-seller *God Doesn't Have a Draft Card,* and his famous "Eat, Drink, and Be Mary" sermon, which celebrated both natural grains and celibacy.

But Father Strum-a-Tune may be a dinosaur in today's world, sitting in his book-lined study fingering well-worn pages of Thoreau and Teilhard de Chardin. Humming "Michael Row the Boat Ashore" and drawing up plans for a geodesic dome church, Father awaits the day when social consciousness will again be raised and his flock will once more march to the beat of a different drummer.

FATHER FRANK HANDS AND THE CHURCH OF HOLY HEALING

THEY ARE LINED UP three rows deep at the front of the church. They are singing and clapping and swaying from side to side. Every few moments someone lets out a wail that sends shivers down your spine. A man approaches and places his hands on a woman's forehead and she immediately pitches backward in a dead faint. Someone is always there to grab the falling body.

No, this isn't West Virginia and there aren't any poisonous snakes being passed around. The scene is a Catholic church in St. Louis and the man doing the touching is Father Frank Hands, the charismatic priest. Lest you suspect otherwise, Father Hands is a real priest, seminary-educated and ordained according to Church regulations. Indeed, his activities are sanctioned by the Church, and that means the Pope.

Father Frank Hands can heal (through the intercession of Jesus Christ, of course), and he has thrilled the Faithful with his amazing powers. The movement is growing, and pretty soon you won't know the difference between the Catholics and the Holy Rollers. Father Hands first learned of his powers as a boy, when his neighbor's pet goldfish died. Little Father Hands snatched the poor beast from the toilet bowl and placed the motionless creature in a plastic bag full of warm water. The next day the goldfish was swimming in furious circles in the bag. Soon the small street in St. Louis looked like Lourdes. People brought pets from all over town to be healed. Although Father

Frank was not as successful with cats and dogs as he was with goldfish, news of the amazing miracle spread.

Last year Father Hands appeared all over the country in front of large crowds (60,000 in Des Moines, 80,000 in Philadelphia) bringing the word to the people. Father Hands realizes that many Catholics are not entirely pleased to have priests running around healing people in quite such a dramatic fashion. They think this smacks of backwoods mumbo jumbo. But as Father Frank Hands is quick to point out, Jesus did a bit of healing Himself, and no one compares him to Oral Roberts.

HOLY VESTMENTS
HOW CLOTHES MAKE THE PRIEST

THE VESTMENTS WORN by priests during Mass each have a special function and meaning. Like army uniforms, they must be worn according to strict regulations. Other clothing worn by priests is generally considered to be "off-duty" wear. Sometimes informal garments, if carefully concealed, can be slipped on un-

der holy garb. The garments displayed below will allow Father to be dressed in a variety of appropriate outfits. As a test of your ecclesiastical knowledge and fashion sense, see if you can dress him so he'll pass muster at Sunday Mass, at the same time allowing for a little individuality and flair. →

COATS OF MANY COLORS

Like a sensible business wardrobe, priestly vestments over the centuries have become pared-down, functional, and yet fundamentally flattering. The sacristy is a dressing room full of classics even more time-honored than the pin-striped suit, the wing-tip shoe, and the trench coat.

There are only five approved colors for the chasuble: white, red, green, violet, and black, although gold may be substituted for green, white, and red under certain circumstances. Test your knowledge of this ancient symbolism by matching each color with its liturgical meaning and appropriate season.

Colors

1. White   3. Green   5. Black
2. Red   4. Violet   6. Gold

Meaning

A. Humility and penance
E. Hope
B. Mourning and sadness
F. Envy
C. Joy and purity
G. A wealthy parish
D. Fire of love toward God

Season

a. Pentecost; feast days of the Apostles and Martyrs
b. Between Pentecost and Advent and from Epiphany to
   Septuagesima
c. Good Friday, All Souls' Day, Masses for the Dead
d. During Advent and Lent
e. Christmas to Epiphany, Eastertide, joyous feast days
f. After Memorial Day and before Labor Day
g. Great solemnities; anytime the Church wants to impress

ANSWERS:
1. C,e; 2. D,a; 3. E,b; 4. A,d; 5. B,c; 6. C,D, or E,g.

THE PRIEST'S WARDROBE

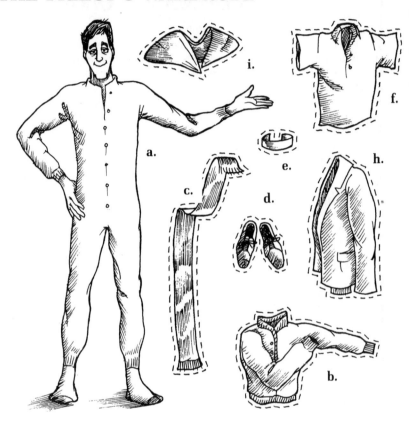

a. Long underwear for chilly winter Masses

b. Hand-knit black cardigan bought on trip to Ireland's holy shrines

c. Cashmere scarf given by grateful parishioner for bringing Communion to her at home when she was in traction

d. Black oxfords

e. Clerical collar

f,g,h. Standard black shirt, pants, and jacket

i. Amice—white linen cloth, covers neck and shoulders. Represents helm of salvation. Recalls the cloth with which Jesus was blindfolded while soldiers struck him.

j. Alb—white linen robe signifying spiritual purity. Also calls to mind the white garment in which Herod had Jesus clothed in order to mock Him.

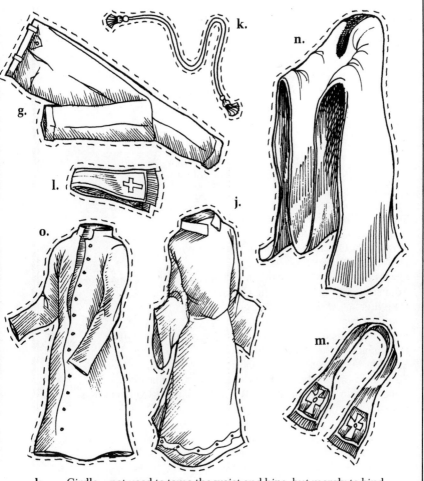

k.   Girdle—not used to tame the waist and hips, but merely to bind the alb around the midsection. Emblem of purity.

l.   Maniple—long piece of cloth worn on the left arm, representing the rewards for good works involving suffering and labor.

m.   Stole—worn around the neck and crossed at the breast. Represents the spiritual powers and dignity of the priest.

n.   Chasuble—symbol of God's charity to men, as well as the priest's own charity, and of the purple robe Jesus was forced to wear when He was crowned with thorns.

o.   Cassock—ankle-length robe, usually black, with close-fitting sleeves. Everyday wear.

HOLY APPELLATIONS!
The Most Colorful Orders of Priests and Nuns

The names and orders of priests and nuns give an indication of the character of the rule. The Sisters tend to stress the mystical while the Fathers take a no-nonsense approach, as you'll see from the following lists.

Nuns

Benedictine Nuns of the Primitive Observance
Carmelite Sisters of St. Thérèse of the Infant Jesus
Daughters of Divine Charity
Little Missionary Sisters of Charity
Sisters of Charity of Our Lady, Mother of Mercy
Cistercian Nuns of the Strict Observance
Servants of Our Lady Queen of the Clergy
Daughters of the Cross
Sisters of the Holy Cross and of the Seven Dolors
Augustinian Daughters of the Crucified
Daughters of St. Francis of Assisi
The Poor Clares
Sister Servants of the Holy Spirit of Perpetual Adoration
Handmaids of the Precious Blood
Servants of the Holy Heart of Mary
Sister Servants of the Holy Ghost and Mary Immaculate
Congregation of the Incarnate Word and the Blessed Sacrament
Nursing Sisters of the Sick Poor
Little Sisters of Jesus
Poor Handmaids of Jesus Christ
Sister Adorers of the Precious Blood
Sisters of Our Lady of Charity of the Refuge
Company of the Savior

Priests

Augustinians	Marist Fathers	Salesians
Benedictines	Maryknoll Fathers	Somascans
Carmelites	Oratorian Fathers	Sulpicians
Cistercians	Pallottines	Trappists
Dominicans	Premonstratensians	Trinitarians
Franciscans	Resurrectionists	Vincentians
Holy Ghost Fathers	Redemptorists	Xaverians
Marian Fathers		

THESE SPLENDID SISTERS

OUR FAVORITE NUNS

Mother Seton and the American Sisters of Charity. Mother Seton was born in 1774 to a family of means and social position in New York. In early life a wife, mother, and Episcopalian, she lost her father and husband to a virulent epidemic and converted to Catholicism. Soon afterward, she founded an order of Sisters to care for those similarly afflicted. Clearly well on her way to sainthood, the Sister saw service during the Civil War. For her devotion, charity, and no doubt war service, she was made the first canonized American saint.

Les Mesdames du Sacré Coeur, or Madames of the Sacred Heart. Founded in France in 1803, this order was brought to the United States in 1818 by Rose Philippine Duchesne. Mme. Duchesne has since been beatified and her body is preserved intact at the St. Charles School in St. Louis. The madames administer some of the most exclusive Catholic girls' schools in the U.S. Each new graduate is presented with a card reading *"Je suis enfant du Sacré Coeur"* ("I am a child of the Sacred Heart"), entitling her to the hospitality and protection of any of the order's institutions throughout the world. It used to be that a clever and perhaps somewhat cynical graduate could wend her way virtually around the globe without ever paying for a hotel room or a meal. With the shrinking of the order's holdings in recent years, however, travel possibilities have become much more limited. The Madames of the Sacred Heart are one of the few orders that allow members to retain their original names.

Mother Cabrini and the Missionary Sisters of the Sacred Heart. Mother Cabrini addressed herself to the welfare of Italian immigrants in America, becoming known as the "Apostle of the Italians." Daughter of a noble Italian family, she opened many houses for the poor and proposed to Pope Leo XIII that she take her Sisters to the Orient. He disagreed and suggested that, like Christopher Columbus, they change their destination and go to the Americas instead. Fortunately for hundreds of thousands of Italian-Americans, she went where she was told and founded many settlement houses and hospitals.

St. Clare and the Franciscan Nuns. Born to a wealthy and knighted family of Assisi, St. Clare was known for her good works and her fine dress. Like the Junior League, she demonstrated that a woman can slave for charity and still look smashing. Underneath the elegant garments befitting her station, however, was a hair shirt to remind St. Clare that she was devoted to the Lord and not to worldly possessions. Accompanied by a chaperone, she would visit Father Francis of Assisi (later St. Francis of Assisi) and receive instruction from him. Following his example, Clare renounced worldly goods. Her family tried everything to make her return to her former way of life, but they failed. St. Clare and her order cut their hair in the tonsure way and set about being Sisters of the Poor. The Pope visited her on her deathbed and granted the order the right to poverty.

St. Scholastica and the Benedictine Nuns. St. Scholastica had a brother named Benedict (later St. Benedict) who was a monk. One day he was visiting her and she asked him to stay a while longer. Benedict, however, was bound by a rule that monks must return to the abbey before nightfall. Scholastica begged him to stay but he refused. She then laid her hands on the table and prayed. A storm arose and it became far too windy for Benedict to return to the abbey that night. This was confirmed by Pope Gregory, who reportedly said, "Hell hath no fury like a woman's storm." St. Scholastica went on to found an order under her brother's rules to enhance intellectual and cultural education for women.

PENNSYLVANIA:
THE NUN STATE

SOME MIGHT QUESTION our designation of Pennsylvania as "The Nun State." "Don't you know," they could say, "that there are over 15,000 nuns in California and only about 5,000 in Pennsylvania?" That may be true. Nevertheless, on car trips across the long wooded state named after William Penn, the state that is home to one of the great Catholic bastions in America, Philadelphia, you will see the signs. The signs say things like, ST. FELICITA HOUSE: HOME OF THE FELICITANS. Those signs at the edge of the highway always seem to be at the entrance to a tree-lined tunnel that appears to lead nowhere. Take the road sometime. At the end, tucked in among the trees, is a charming building that looks like part of a small university gone to seed. You might have expected to discover a gingerbread house, but what you have found is a motherhouse.

The motherhouse is home base, *terra firma,* the Emerald City of a given order of nuns. This is where the Mother Superior keeps track of her order and where the elderly nun can find a quiet place to spend her remaining days after her mission in the world is at an end. Certain nuns never leave the motherhouse at all. They are called "cloistered," even though they rarely live in anything resembling a cloister. Next time you are talking to your favorite nun, ask her if she ever spent any time in Pennsylvania at a motherhouse. The answer, more often than not, will be yes.

Why there seem to be more of these motherhouses in Pennsylvania than in other states is a mystery. On your next drive through keep your eyes peeled, and instead of playing license plate games count how many signs for motherhouses there are. No fair pretending you didn't see the sign that says "Welcome to New Jersey" while continuing to count.

NUNS WE HAVE KNOWN

SIMPLY PUT, the teaching nuns can be classified in two distinct camps: the nice nuns and the mean nuns. But as anyone surviving parochial school can attest, there are as many nun types as there are Beatitudes. Maybe more. Herewith, a roundup of the most common.

THE PIOUS NUN

This nun believes that anything can be solved by saying a Rosary. Her class prays collectively before class, at lunch, after recess, and at the end of the day. Special prayers are said before tests, during Lent, and on Holy Days. The time Sister lost her grading chart, the whole day was spent offering up prayers to St. Anthony. The pious nun is often an older nun with a sweet, saintly disposition. We all know she's going straight to Heaven.

THE ATHLETIC NUN

She wields a softball bat with prowess and serves a volleyball with a wallop. The athletic nun can be found teaching phys. ed. in many parochial schools. She often takes the name of a fearless male saint, i.e., Sister Stephen Anne, Sister Mary Daniel. She was one of the first to adopt modern garb. This nun is nice, but strict. Even the eighth-grade boys are afraid of her.

THE ANCIENT NUN

Many years ago she was surely an effective, responsive teacher,

but those days have come and gone. Sister uses yellowed notes and doesn't notice when her students move the hands of the classroom clock forward to recess time. Every parochial school child has had an ancient nun as a teacher, and every student looks back on that year as the jolliest ever.

THE ULTIMATE NUN

Most parochial schools have a nun that every child adores. She's somewhat strict, but always fair. The ultimate nun likes field trips and will take the class to places like the Coca-Cola bottling plant instead of a boring museum. She goes to all the basketball games and cheers loudly. Everyone wants to sit next to her and cheer, too. Some ultimate nuns can even play the guitar.

THE STRICT NUN

Watch out! According to this nun, every thought, word, or action will land you one step closer to Hell. Solution: Don't think, talk, or do anything unless you absolutely have to, and then be careful. *Never* raise your hand in class, even when you think you know the answer. It's not worth the risk of getting yelled at or rapped on the knuckles. Children taught by a strict nun tend to lapse into panicked silent prayer regularly, and shoot sharp, darting glances around the classroom, keeping an eye on Sister's whereabouts. Parents should watch for early signs of ulcers.

THE YOUNG NUN

A rare breed these days. She is sometimes plain, sometimes beautiful, but always perky and enthusiastic. The young nun is a lot like Maria von Trapp. The other teachers like her because she doesn't mind daily cafeteria duty.

TRUE CONFESSIONS
BELIEVE-IT-OR-NOT NUN STORIES

SISTER MARY BERNARD

One day a pigeon flew into Sr. Mary Bernard's fifth-grade classroom in a suburb of Detroit. Perhaps it had been attracted by the bread crusts that the children, encouraged by Sr. Mary Bernard, had placed on the windowsills as an act of kindness toward God's wild creatures. The ancient nun had been showing signs of encroaching senility for some time, but the children were taken aback when she clutched her hands to her breast, made a hurried Sign of the Cross, and ordered them to kneel by their desks. As all eyes followed the panicked bird flapping its way wildly around the room, Sister informed the class that a miracle had taken place. The Holy Spirit had descended, she said, and they would have to remain in a kneeling position until the Bishop arrived to confirm it. Fortunately, one of the children was sent to fetch the principal, Sr. Clothilde, who told the children to take their seats and assured Sr. Mary Bernard that she personally would take the matter up with the Bishop. The next day the children returned to find a substitute teacher. Sr. Mary Bernard never returned to the classroom.

SISTER CLARE

As every nun knew, school dances were among the nearest of Near Occasions of Sin. Every precaution was taken to ensure that lustful thoughts would not be incited. Girls were required to kneel upon entering the gym to prove that their hems would touch the floor. Gowns were required to have straps (even if spaghetti-skinny), and patent-leather shoes were out. For the ride to and from the dance, girls were encouraged to carry a phone book (to perch upon in case they had to sit on a boy's lap) and a dime to place between their knees. If it fell to the floor, they were to use it to call their parents. Once the music got under way, chaperones circulated around the dance floor, making sure that couples left room for the Holy Spirit between them. For Sister Clare, principal of a high school in Cleveland, however, these precautions were not enough. At the end of every dance, she would require her students to kneel and say an Act of Contrition for the sinful thoughts she was certain they must have had.

SISTER THERESA

In her declining years, Sr. Theresa found it difficult to keep up a full day's teaching schedule in her sixth-grade classroom near Dallas. After lunch, she would direct the boys to read silently from their geography texts, while the girls were instructed to crochet or do needlepoint, the results of which Sr. Theresa would eventually collect and give away as Christmas presents. Two Hispanic girls who knew no English spent the entire day doing handicrafts, producing particularly splendid creations. While her students were thus engaged, Sr. Theresa herself would watch soap operas all afternoon, the black-and-white portable on her desk carefully angled so that only she could see the screen. Occasionally she would spend the afternoon in the cloakroom, carefully starching and ironing the articles her pupils had created, emerging only to rub blue, sticky starch in the face of a mis-

behaving child. The children did not think to question this routine, or anything else a nun did, in those pre–Vatican II days. Eventually a few parents gathered what was going on, however, and there was reform. From that point on, both boys and girls were given silent reading assignments to last the afternoon, and Sister's only "Guiding Light" came from Heaven above.

SISTER MARGUERITE

During a discussion of career possibilities, one of Sr. Marguerite's eighth-grade boys in Philadelphia had an upset stomach. Knowing he would be refused permission to go to the rest room until the period ended, he tried to ignore the heaving in his middle. Alas, the flu bug got the better of him and he threw up on the floor by his desk. Sr. Marguerite quickly put an end to the minor uproar that ensued. "Now, how many of you said you wanted to be nurses?" she queried, and several girls tentatively raised their hands. "Well, Mary Elizabeth," she said to the most pious of the bunch, "why don't you go get some paper towels and clean up the floor. You're going to be doing a lot of unpleasant things like this as a nurse, and you might as well start learning now."

EYES IN THE BACK OF HER HEAD:

THE NUN'S POINT OF VIEW

THE LEGEND PERSISTS that nuns have a sort of sixth sense in the classroom, an uncanny ability to detect even the smallest infraction of the rules, almost as if they had eyes in the back of their heads. Here is one nun's account of how she went about establishing this legend among her students:

I was substituting for a few days for a Sister who'd taken a much-needed spiritual retreat. I'd heard that this particular class was a rough group, and I knew I'd have to take control right away, otherwise the classroom would have been a living . . . well, I would have had to go on a spiritual retreat myself. As I approached the classroom, I could hear a sort of dull, ugly roar even in the hallway, as if several Christian martyrs had just been thrown to the lions. If ever I were to join their hallowed ranks, I vowed, it would not be that day.

As I proceeded to my desk at the front of the room, I main-tained a steely silence. With a stiff wimple under my chin, I couldn't help but hold my head high and proud. And the long black veil hanging down over the sides of my face kept the little hooligans from seeing that I was glancing discreetly around the classroom, searching for anything that would help me not merely to survive, but to prevail, in this most hostile of environments.

Out of the corner of my eye, I noticed a wadded-up piece of paper—by the sticky look of it, a humongous spitball—lying on the floor near a desk in the back row. Before proceeding to the blackboard to write out my name and the day's assignments, I glanced at the alphabetical seating plan. The student nearest to the spitball was Malone, Thomas. Naturally, Tommy Malone was not the student in that seat at the moment. After all, I didn't take my vows yesterday. Mixing up the new Sister by playing musical chairs was the oldest trick in the book.

As I began to write "JMJ" at the

top of the board, I said casually, "I hope everyone is in the correct seat. Because I have some special after-school work in the church neatening up candle wicks for anyone who isn't in the right seat by the time I finish writing out this assignment." After the shuffling and scraping died down, I kept on writing for several more minutes, never once looking back at the class. Just as I was finishing up, I said in the same offhand tone of voice as before, "Would Thomas Malone please pick up the piece of paper lying next to his desk and deposit it in the wastebasket?"

As I turned around, a loutish lad with an awestruck look on his face lumbered down the aisle and reverently placed the wad in the can. From there on in, I had very few problems.

Nuns Say The Darndest Things:

"No."
"Woe betide you!"
"Bold and brazen."
"Kiss it up to God."
"Offer it up."
"You're putting another nail in the Cross."
"Line up in size order."
"You're my cross to bear."
"I'll just wait until you're ready. We have all day."
"Did you bring enough gum for everyone in the class?"
"Keep your eyes off your neighbor's paper."
"No."

CATHOLIC FUN FACTS

Roman Collars on the Comeback Trail. There was a blessed increase in the number of Priests, up by 21 from the previous year. Bishops were up by 22. Deacons soared by 636, but Brothers were down 62 in mixed trading.

FOUR

UPON THIS ROCK

THE APOSTLE

The Apostles were the ones who were there in the beginning, flawed but loving followers of Our Lord. What is really known about these

Name	Hails From	Occupation
Peter	Galilee	Fisherman
Andrew	Galilee	Fisherman
Thomas	Galilee	Unemployed
James (The Less)	Galilee	Unemployed
James (The Greater)	Galilee	Fisherman
Bartholomew	Galilee	Unemployed
Simon the Canaanite	Galilee	Unemployed
Matthew	Galilee	Tax Collector
Phillip	Galilee	Unemployed
John	Galilee	Fisherman
Jude	Galilee	Unemployed
Judas Iscariot	Southern Judea	Business Management

FACT SHEET

first envoys and disciples? The following fact sheet will fill in any gaps in knowledge you may have about the original Apostles.

Favorite Saying	Will Be Remembered For
"I don't know him. I really don't!"	Being our Rock, the first Pope
"Any wine left?"	Being the first Apostle
"You expect me to believe that!"	Doubting
"Less filling!"	Being thrown to his death from the top of the temple in Jerusalem
"Tastes great!"	First Apostle to die by the sword
"It doesn't get any better than this."	Being flayed
"You can call me the Canaanite or you can call me the Zealot."	Being sawed in two
"That will put us in a higher tax bracket!"	Writing a Gospel
"Huh?"	Being there
"I was always the favorite."	Writing a Gospel and living to be 100.
"When you call me don't say 'Hey Jude!' "	Writing shortest Epistle
"Stand by me."	Being the first to trade in silver

PUZZLERS

CATHOLIC BRAIN PUZZLER #1

Jesus is teaching in front of a huge crowd and it is getting close to supper time. The Apostles ask the people in the crowd, which numbers about 50,000, to share their food. After a collection is taken, the Apostles find there are only a few loaves of bread and a couple of dried fishes. Jesus begins handing out the food and it turns out that all 50,000 people get fed.

Q. How many loaves and fishes did each person in the crowd get for dinner?

Q. What did everyone eat for dessert?

CATHOLIC BRAIN PUZZLER #2

A man has a vineyard. It is twenty acres by forty acres. He hires men to work at eight o'clock in the morning and agrees to pay them fifty piasters for a day's work. At noon he goes out and hires more men and agrees to pay them fifty piasters for a half-day's work also. The men who were hired in the morning complain that this is not fair. The vineyard owner says, "The first shall be last and the last shall be first."

Q. Why do the people who came late get paid the same amount as those who worked all day?
Q. How many grapes are there in the vineyard?

CATHOLIC BRAIN PUZZLER #3

A king once invited all his friends to his son's wedding feast. The son was a prince. However, none of the people invited would come. Then the king instructed his servants to go out and invite both "good and bad" men. The rented hall was soon full of revelers. When the king came to the hall, he saw that one of the guests was not dressed properly. He instructed his servants to throw him out.

Q. Since the king obviously wasn't too picky about whom he invited, why did he get so upset when someone showed up improperly dressed?
Q. Why didn't anyone want to come to the feast in the first place? Was Sinatra singing at Radio City Music Hall?

CATHOLIC BRAIN PUZZLER #4

A man once invited all his friends to a great supper. But all the friends made excuses as to why they could not come. One said there was a new play in town that he had to see. Another said he had to wash his camel. So the man told his servants to go out and invite the sick, poor, and lame to the feast. They all came and had a great dinner.

Q. What was the man serving for dinner?
Q. Did the man who gave the dinner know the king from Brain Puzzler #3?

God Is Not A Baseball Fan

In the 1985 World Series, which could have been billed as The Church vs. The State Series instead of the I-90 Series, the Kansas City Royals defeated the St. Louis Cardinals in seven games. Lest there by any doubt that this lack of divine intervention was intentional, we need only look at the 1984 Series, which saw the Detroit Tigers devour the San Diego Padres.

God Is A Football Fan

Mike Ditka, head coach for the 1986 World Champion Chicago Bears football team, praying for divine intervention during the Super Bowl. His and all of Chicago's prayers were answered with a 46–10 victory over the New England Patriots.

IN OUR TIME
THE NEW SACRAMENTS

Q. WHAT IS A SACRAMENT?

A. A sacrament is an outward sign instituted by Christ to give grace.

FULL OF POMP and circumstance, pre–Vatican II sacraments conjured up feelings of fear and unworthiness, which were only slightly buffered by the otherworldly image of God's cleansing grace sprinkling down upon our sullied souls.

Unbelievable as it may sound, radical changes have taken place in the sacraments we've known and loved. One supposes the desire was to make the sacraments more accessible, communal, and uplifting. But some Catholics who were just beginning to feel comfortable with pre-Confession sweaty palms and the dread of ever having to pull out the dusty sick-call set are feeling cheated. Their beloved sacraments have been watered down and wimped up. The transformation has been shrewdly gradual (did they think no one would notice?), and it's taken some parishes decades to effect the gross modifications called for.

BAPTISM

Baptism is still, thank God, called Baptism, but the ceremony has become more like a baby pageant than a sacrament. Infants are now baptized en masse, which means that parents are comparing pricy christening gowns while babies are comparing vocal capacities. Unless you are a parent or godparent, offer to skip the ceremony and stay home to mix up the ginger ale punch for the reception.

CONFESSION

Confession is now called The Sacrament of Reconciliation, which sounds more like patching up an argument with a pal than partaking in one of the sacraments. Participants receive it in a group, without ever having to memorize prayers or humiliate themselves by reciting their sins aloud. But can God truly be forgiving without the recipient enduring the terror of old-time sessions in the confessional? If mumbling a few apologetic prayers in a church full of fellow sinners doesn't make you feel like you've come clean, say the prayers twice and throw an extra ten dollars in the collection basket. There now, feel better?

EXTREME UNCTION

In past years, Extreme Unction, also known less formally as The Last Sacrament, was the most somber of sacraments. Few Catholics knew what Extreme Unction meant and fewer still knew that it was two words. Priests rose silently in the still of the night and rushed to the bedsides of dying parishioners to administer the Last Rites (another name for the same sacrament).

HOLY NUMBERS

1. Precepts
2. Capital sins
3. Commandments
4. Beatitudes
5. Stations of the Cross
6. Mysteries
7. Holy Days of Obligation
8. Sacraments
9. Hail Marys in a Rosary
10. Parishes in the United States

a. seven
b. eight
c. fifteen
d. six
e. fifty-three
f. 19,118
g. fourteen
h. ten
i. six (in the U.S.)
j. seven

ANSWERS:
1. d; 2. j; 3. h; 4. b; 5. g; 6. c; 7. i; 8. a; 9. e; 10. f.

These days, anyone can receive what is now called The Sacrament of the Sick, whether for a serious disease, a lingering flu bug, or a nasty paper cut. Some hypochondriacal Catholics even regard the Sacrament of the Sick as a sort of supplemental health insurance. If you receive it once, the sacrament is supposed to last until you really need it, although many Catholics would feel less apprehensive about the trip to the Pearly Gates with a booster on their deathbeds.

Standard, Always Acceptable Confessions To Use Anytime

Do you find examining your conscience tedious and time-consuming? Here's the answer to your prayers. Simply memorize the appropriate confession and repeat it each time you go to Confession.

CHILD
- disobeyed
- fought with brothers and sisters
- stole candy bar
- took the Lord's name in vain

TEENAGER
- lied to parents
- took the Lord's name in vain
- impure thoughts
- lied to Sister about attending CYO meeting
- general surliness

YOUNG ADULT
- missed Mass
- lied to parents
- padded newly acquired expense account
- impure thoughts
- impure acts and miscellaneous

PARENT
- lied to children
- intentionally went over credit card limit
- lied at Weight Watchers meeting
- weaseled out of volunteering for United Way
- sent store-bought cake to parish bake sale; accepted compliments heartily
- threw away bazaar raffle tickets instead of selling them
- donated only unpleasant canned goods—i.e., beets, creamed corn, succotash—to annual church drive

GRANDPARENT
- lied to grandchildren
- cheated at Bingo—yelled too early, acted confused, got to keep prize
- did not discuss fund-raising project at Rosary Guild meeting; too busy discussing fashions on "Dynasty"
- compared friends' grandchildren unfavorably to my own
- uncharitable thoughts about dawdling delivery boy from Meals on Wheels

Clip 'N' Save!!

MODERN SIN

When Moses hurled the tablets down from atop Mount Sinai, he had no conception of the complexities that Catholics of the 1980s would face in attempting to keep the Ten Commandments. Go to Confession immediately if any of the following apply to you.

Sin

Commandment Broken

Bootleg movies on your VCR.

Thou shall not steal.

Worship that shiny new Porsche of yours.

I am the Lord thy God, thou shalt not have strange gods before Me.

As the neighbor of the fellow with the Porsche, be extremely jealous.

Thou shalt not covet thy neighbor's goods.

Swear lustily when the Cuisinart blade takes off the tip of your index finger.

Thou shalt not take the name of the Lord thy God in vain.

Be tempted when your next-door neighbor's wife, a cute aerobics instructor, makes a pass at you.

Thou shalt not covet they neighbor's wife.

Since you forgot to put on the snow tires, decide that it's too dangerous to drive to Mass.

Remember to keep holy the Sabbath.

Serve goat cheese, which you know your mother loathes, at a family gathering.

Honor thy father and thy mother.

CHURCH LATIN
IT'S ALL GREEK TO ME

BEFORE VATICAN II, the Mass was said in Latin. For many centuries, the priest did all the talking, but eventually the congregation got to chime in as well. Since Latin was a language that very few of them understood, the only way they could do this was to learn their set responses phonetically, the way the Miss Universe contestants from many countries would learn the English words to the poignant pageant theme song. The resulting utterances—during both contest and Mass—were similarly odd-sounding.

True, the Church did provide Latin-English missals so that the Faithful would know what they and the priest were saying. These ecclesiastical Berlitz guides were of little practical use, however, since the priest usually spoke so rapidly, so softly, and with such a bad accent that one couldn't tell exactly where he was. It didn't help that his back was to the congregation most of the time as he faced the altar.

The Mass in translation, like many a subtitled foreign movie, was hard to follow. Only a few phrases from the Latin Mass really penetrated the consciousness of most Catholics, usually for all the wrong reasons. The following is a list of these select phrases, why we remember them, and what their real meaning to us was.

"In nomine Patris, et Filii, et Spiritus Sancti."

Translation: *"In the name of the Father, and of the Son, and of the Holy Spirit."*

This was the kickoff, the very first thing the priest said, and so only a few members of the congregation had gotten lost by this point, or were there to hear it.

"Sicut erat in principio, et nunc, et semper: et in saecula saeculorum. Amen."

"As it was in the beginning, is now and ever shall be: world without end. Amen."

This phrase punctuated the Mass periodically, providing a familiar signpost amid all the unfamiliar verbiage. Like the occasional Howard Johnson's restaurant along a bleak stretch of interstate highway, it meant progress was being made, however tediously. Amen. The *"in saecula saeculorum"* part was particularly memorable because of the alliteration.

"In nomine Domini."

"In the name of the Lord."

Another phrase to delight the ear. Rhyming words always made things much easier.

"Confiteor Deo omnipotenti . . ."

"I confess to almighty God . . ."

The Latin Mass might be compared to a business meeting. After a bit of chitchat and a series of respectful introductions, it was time to get down to the nitty-gritty, and of course the first item on the agenda was Our Sins. The Confiteor is a long sequence. It is the original "litany of errors."

"Mea culpa, mea culpa, mea maxima culpa."

"Through my fault, through my fault, through my most grievous fault."

This was the culmination of the Confiteor, where everyone got to strike his breast three times on the strong beat. It is also a perfect illustration of the real reason why Catholics have so much guilt: because the Church made

it all seem so glamorous. Those who doubt this should take note of the following rapturous excerpt from a Missal used in the 1950s: "A dramatic picture indeed! humbly striking our breast, symbol of stirring up conscience, of disciplining body and soul; first confessing our sins publicly, then beseeching grace and help from God, the Church in heaven and on earth."

"Misereatur vestri omnipotens Deus . . ."

"May almighty God have mercy upon you . . ."

It was the part that sounded like "misery" that caught the ear, since this was what you were often feeling by this point. The bonus was that you felt you were doing Penance merely by attending, as well as fulfilling the weekly Obligation.

"Gloria in Excelsis Deo."

"Glory to God in the Highest."

You knew this one because it was the refrain to the lovely Christmas hymn of the same name, also known as "Angels We Have Heard on High."

"Kyrie Eleison."

"Lord, have mercy."

Not Latin at all, but Greek. The beginning of a very moving chant. This became the title of a rock-and-roll hymn sung by the Byrds in the 1960s, used in the soundtrack of the film *Easy Rider*. A song called "Kyrie" by the band Mr. Mister became a hit in 1986.

"Dominus vobiscum."
"Et cum spiritu tuo."
"Oremus."

> *"The Lord be with you."*
> *"And with your spirit."*
> *"Let us pray."*

This was the most familiar set piece of the entire Mass, repeated again and again. We wondered how many times we had to be reminded the Lord was with us. Once He arrived, wouldn't He stay for a while? *"Et cum spiritu tuo,"* contrary to popular belief, was not the rectory phone number. *"Oremus"* meant "Here we go again."

"Sanctus, sanctus, sanctus . . ."

> *"Holy, holy, holy . . ."*

The lovely repetition got 'em every time.

"Per Christum Dominum Nostrum."

> *"Through Christ Our Lord."*

A lot of "ums."

"Per Ipsum, et Cum Ipso, et In Ipso."

> *"Through Him, with Him, and in Him."*

A real Latin tongue twister.

"Ite, Missa est."
"Deo gratias."

> *"Go, the Mass is ended."*
> *"Thanks be to God."*

You said it. *"Deo gratias"* gets by far the heartiest response of the day.

NAME THAT HYMN

A. "And humbly I'll receive Thee, the Bridegroom of my soul"

B. "Sweet Sacrament! We Thee adore. Oh make us love Thee more and more"

C. *"Fit panis hominum: Dat panis coelicus!"*

D. "Near thee, Madonna, fondly we hover"

E. "Our hearts are on fire"

F. "O Mary we crown Thee with blossoms today"

G. *"O piissima"*

H. *"Quae coeli pandis hostium"*

I. *"Veneremur cernui"*

J. *"Gló-ó-o-o-o-ó-ó-o-o-o-ó-ó-o-o-o-ó-ria, in excelsis Deo"*

K. "Milk and honey on the other side"

Somethin' From the Oven: The Whole-Wheat Host

The origins of the whole-wheat Communion host are dubious. Perhaps its invention stems from an increased emphasis on nutrition, or possibly it was developed in reaction to uprisings of disgruntled Catholics revolting against thin white hosts glued to the roofs of their mouths.

In any case, host factories have begun turning out hearty-grained hosts in record numbers. The same size as traditional hosts, they are thicker and have a chewier texture, making the process of transferring the host from tongue to stomach all the more manageable. (It's generally accepted these days that chewing the host is okay.)

The following is a recipe for the basic whole-wheat Communion host. Show it to your pastor if your parish still uses the old-fashioned wafers.

INGREDIENTS

½ cup warm milk
¼ cup honey
¼ cup oil
2 cups whole-wheat flour
1 tsp. salt

PROCEDURE

In mixing bowl combine milk, honey, and oil. Sift the flour and salt and add to the liquids and mix thoroughly. With a rolling pin, roll the dough to a thickness of ⅛ inch. Using a small round cookie cutter or the rim of a shot glass, cut the dough into as many circles as possible. Roll out the dough again and cut more rounds. Place hosts on an oiled baking sheet and bake at 350° for 10 minutes. Store in a covered container.

Makes 100 hosts.

1. On This Day, O Beautiful Mother
2. O Lord, I Am Not Worthy
3. *O Salutaris Hostia*
4. Angels We Have Heard on High
5. *O Sanctissima*
6. Jesus, My Lord, My God, My All
7. Michael, Row Your Boat Ashore
8. Immaculate Mary
9. *Tantum Ergo*
10. *Panis Angelicus*
11. Bring Flowers of the Rarest

MY FIRST HYMNAL

FAVORITE CATHOLIC HYMNS

Arranged

FOR PIANO

by

ADA RICHTER

McLaughlin & Reilly Co Boston, Mass

LIKE A VIRGIN? NAY!

THE BISHOP'S LETTER ON MADONNA

FROM TIME TO TIME there appears in popular culture a figure whose influence among Catholic youth is so controversial that it is incumbent upon Church leaders to comment. Such a figure is Madonna, the singer whose music and fashions have had a sensational effect throughout our society.

Madonna's name brings to mind the Blessed Mother, but unfortunately the similarity ends there. Naming a child Madonna under any circumstances is questionable, if not exactly blasphemous, and for this the superstar's parents must be held accountable. It is up to Madonna herself to decide how to honor her hallowed name, however, and so far her actions have not been encouraging.

As far as we know, the Blessed Mother was always modestly attired, generally in a gown of pastel blue. Madonna, however, seems to have a penchant for black undergarments that would hardly be appropriate for any Catholic woman of virtue, let alone a self-proclaimed virgin on a public stage. It is her use of Crucifixes and Rosary beads as earrings, necklaces, brooches, and other forms of adornment, however, that is most disturbing. Granted, the Blessed Mother did not have the opportunity to wear Rosary beads and Crucifixes, as these did not become objects of

veneration until after her Assumption into Heaven. We doubt, however, that she would have worn them with the same sort of carefree abandon that Madonna exhibits.

If we could talk to Madonna in her own language, it would go something like this: "Come on, Material Girl, you have already crossed the Borderline of bad taste. The world may be Crazy for You, but you must decide whether you are a Boy Toy or truly Like a Virgin. You may be married now (was it a Catholic ceremony, by the way?), but you are still an example to millions of young girls. Get into the Groove, have your costume designers Dress You Up in something decent, put the Crucifix up over your bed, and save the Rosary for church."

FASHION WITH A CATHOLIC ACCENT

PALMS

At Mass on Palm Sunday, which even the most marginal Catholics attend, palms are given to the faithful as a reminder of Christ's triumphal entry into Jerusalem, when palms were strewn in his path and people cried "Hosanna." Palm Sunday, one week before Easter, commemorates this day. Though long fronds are frequently seen entwined in a Crucifix, draped around holy pictures, or hung over a bed—where they are reputed to act as a lightning repellent—palm also has a favorite use as a fashion accessory. This boutonniere-like article calls for small lengths of palm to be tied in the shape of a cross and affixed (traditionally with a straight pin) to the lapel. The effect is charming, though somewhat ostentatious, and does not show up well against camel hair.

CROSSES

Surprisingly, these are not often seen gracing the breasts of the truly pious. (They prefer the Miraculous Medal.) However, the cross is probably the most ubiquitous Catholic symbol, worn indiscriminately by devout and lapsed alike. It became more popular among men when the open-shirted look came in. On women, it has always been proudly worn outside the blouse or sweater. Though wooden crosses began to appear after Vatican II, this article is most usually seen in gold, excepting those owned by members of the clergy. Sisters, Brothers, and Catholics from warmer climes tend to exaggerate the proportions of this accessory. It is the perfect gift for a godchild.

ROSARIES

These are among the most subtle and inconspicuous of all religious accessories. Though small children tend to wear them around the neck, they are more properly carried in the pocket or purse—unless of course you are a Sister, in which case you are free to tie them around the waist. This style of wear accentuates the beads' provocative aural dimension, which is ordinarily confined to the slight clicking sound Rosaries produce when jingled among coins. Rosary beads provide us with the opportunity to test our knowledge of the Mysteries, as well as to recite the moving Hail Holy Queen, which is rarely said otherwise. They are a favorite First Communion gift, and are usually bought in bulk

on trips to the Vatican; consequently, most Catholics have several. They are available in wood, glass, and two varieties of plastic: ordinary and glow-in-the-dark.

MIRACULOUS MEDALS

When the Blessed Virgin appeared to St. Catherine Labouré standing on a globe, crushing a serpent under her foot, and with rays of light streaming from her hands, she left nothing to St. Catherine's imagination. "Have a medal struck after this model," the Blessed Virgin said. To be sure St. Catherine understood, she added, "They should wear it around the neck." And millions do. Although Miraculous Medals are among the prettiest accents in a fashion-conscious Catholic's collection (often sporting a clear blue veneer over the image of Mary), they are usually worn discreetly and by the truly devout. Since the Virgin promised

Ring Around the Rosary

Q. *What is five decades long, but lasts only half an hour?*
A. The Rosary.

From the early fifteenth century, the Rosary has evolved into a vocal and mental prayer incorporating beads for 6 Our Fathers, 53 Hail Marys, 5 Glory Bes, one Apostles' Creed, and one Hail Holy Queen (which is said at the medal connecting the circle of decades to the little tail with the Crucifix at the end).

When the Rosary is being said in a large church by a large group of people, an interesting audio phenomenon develops. One side of the church tends to get ahead of the other, and pretty soon the cacophony sounds like the Rosary is being said in rounds.

Many Catholic families pray the Rosary together at bedtime, with pajama-clad children kneeling at bedside. But when you have a free moment, don't forget that a decade or two can be offered up when you're in the dentist's waiting room or in a bank line. And even if you don't actually *say* the Rosary, it makes a nice set of worry beads.

to give grace to those whose necks the medals adorn, an element of sincerity is involved in their selection over a strand of pearls or a gold chain. They are frequently given to young Catholic women by young Catholic men.

SCAPULARS

These are worn neither for their beauty nor for their comfort, but for the promise of Heaven given to anyone who wears one until death. Though many will try, none will succeed. Made of wool, string, and two holy pictures encased in plastic, along the lines of a hair shirt, they are extremely irritating and itchy. With that plastic scratching your skin front and back, it is easier to take your chances. The only people who saw the promise of the scapular fulfilled died tragically before they could get it off.

The Holy Mysteries

From the list below, can you pick out the Five Joyful Mysteries? The Five Sorrowful Mysteries? The Five Glorious Mysteries? The Sorrowful ones are a dead giveaway, but the line between Joyful and Glorious is tantalizingly thin.

1. The Annunciation
2. The Carrying of the Cross
3. The Ascension of Our Lord into Heaven
4. The Coronation of Our Blessed Mother in Heaven
5. The Birth of Our Lord
6. The Finding of Our Lord in the Temple
7. The Scourging at the Pillar
8. The Assumption of Our Blessed Mother into Heaven
9. The Visitation
10. The Crucifixion and Death of Our Lord
11. The Descent of the Holy Ghost upon the Apostles
12. The Presentation of Our Lord in the Temple
13. The Crowning with Thorns
14. The Resurrection of Our Lord
15. The Agony of Our Lord in the Garden

Joyful: 1, 9, 5, 12, 6. *Sorrowful:* 15, 7, 13, 2, 10. *Glorious:* 14, 3, 11, 8, 4.
ANSWERS

CATHOLIC CRAFTS

SACRED PALM CRUCIFIX

You will need:
  Sacred palms
  Penknife
  Straight pins

Procedure:
  1. Cut two pieces of palm, one approximately one inch long, the other approximately two inches long.
  2. Slice two openings lengthwise about a third of the way down the longer piece of palm.
  3. Thread the other through the openings to make a cross.
  4. Secure on your lapel with a straight pin.

BACKYARD GROTTO

You will need:
  Large ceramic statue (the Virgin Mary is especially nice)
  Rough-hewn timber
  Hammer, nails, saw
  Rocks, running water, and floodlights (optional)

Procedure:
  1. Build the grotto by nailing slabs of timber together. Don't be concerned if the structure looks rickety; it's more authentic that way.
  2. Secure the statue on a pedestal in the center of the grotto.
  3. If desired, arrange a rock garden and cascading water. Multihued floodlights and piped-in music add a dramatic touch.

ADVENT WREATH

You will need:
  Styrofoam wreath base
  Pine branches
  One pink candle
  Three purple candles

Procedure:
  1. Twist the pine branches around the Styrofoam base.
  2. Insert the candles.
  3. Be careful with the matches.

SPIRITUAL BOUQUET

You will need:
  Construction paper
  Crayons or colored pencils
  Lace, flower stickers, holy cards, doilies, etc.

Procedure:

1. Determine how much praying you are willing to do for the recipient of the Spiritual Bouquet.

2. Fold the paper into a card and write a little verse or prayer. (If the rhyme doesn't come easily, don't force it.) Include the prayers, Masses, and Rosaries you promise to offer up.

3. Decorate the card gaily.

4. If you are all thumbs, buy a Mass card instead.

RONZONI ROSARY

You will need:

Large- and small-size macaroni

String (or dental floss)

Gold spray paint

Small Crucifix

Procedure:

1. String the macaroni, using ten of the small size for Hail Marys and one large size in between the decades. Also use a large-size macaroni to separate the three Hail Marys at the beginning of the Rosary.

2. Spray the whole thing with gold paint.

3. Tie crucifix on the end.

CATHOLIC FUN FACTS

Casting Call Vatican Radio reported an investigation into alleged apparitions to six children by the Virgin Mary near Medjugorje, Yugoslavia. Movie rights are currently available for option. We see Michael J. Fox in the lead role, with Drew Barrymore as his little sister.

I Get Around: Catholics on the Move

Can you match each person to his or her appropriate mode of transportation?

1. altar boy	a. black sedan
2. nun	b. ark
3. priest	c. bulletproof convertible limo
4. former priest	d. beat-up bicycle
5. Pope	e. snazzy sports car
6. Mary and Joseph	f. station wagon
7. Noah	g. donkey

ANSWERS: 1. d; 2. f; 3. a; 4. e; 5. c; 6. g; 7. b.

YOU CAN TAKE HIS WORD FOR IT:

THE INFALLIBILITY OF THE POPE

THE ISSUE OF the infallibility of the Pope has started wars, created rival churches, and even confused some Catholics, but the rules of infallibility are actually pretty simple.

The Pope is considered infallible when he speaks on spiritual topics of "faith and morals," *ex cathedra*—by virtue of his office as Pope—with the assistance of St. Peter (also referred to as speaking from the "Chair of St. Peter"). Simple enough?

But the notion of infallibility has been a continuing source of confusion for Catholics and non-Catholics alike. Take this test and find out what your "Infallibility Quotient" is.

IQ TEST

Example:

	infallible	fallible
If the Pope says:		
A. Rin Tin Tin is the first dog saint.		x
B. Christ is the Son of God.	x	

	INFALLIBLE	FALLIBLE
If the Pope says:		
1. The Blessed Virgin is the Mother of God.		
2. Christ died on the cross and rose again three days later.		
3. The New York Giants will win next year's Super Bowl.		
4. Priests must not marry.		
5. Sean Penn and Madonna must not marry.		
6. There are three distinct beings in one in the Holy Trinity.		
7. The Olympics should be held every five years instead of every four.		
8. Mary is the only person to have been blessed by a Virgin Birth.		
9. Dustin Hoffman should be made an honorary Catholic for his role in *Tootsie*.		
10. God always was and always will be.		

ANSWERS: 1. I; 2. I; 3. F; 4. I; 5. F; 6. I; 7. F; 8. I; 9. F; 10. I

MY TRIP TO THE VATICAN

by Margaret Kelly, Sixth Grade

The Vatican is an extremely big and pretty place. It is a very long walk across the front yard to the door of St. Peter's, but it is made that way so a lot of people can fit in to hear the Pope talk from his balcony. You have to dress nice to go in—no miniskirts. The best parts of it are the bodies of the dead popes all around the church in glass coffins, the bits of St. Peter's chains from when the Romans had him prisoner, the big statues on top which you can see close up if you walk all the way to the roof, and the store, where you can buy Rosaries with pieces of the True Cross or holy water in them, pictures of the Pope, medals, statues, and giant pencils. All of these things have been blessed by the Pope, which makes them better. Outside they sell ice cream and there are men in funny costumes, just like at Disneyland. If you're lucky you get to see the Pope. He comes into the church and talks in ten different languages, only it's hard to tell which one is English. Then he blesses you. This is the most important thing of all. You even get a certificate that says he did, and that means that you will go straight to Heaven when you die if you have the certificate with you. Pretty good for the price of a plane ticket to Rome.

THE GUARDIAN ANGEL
"A Top Catholic Magazine"

CONTENTS

A WORD FROM ME
by
FR. BILL

MANY OF YOU HAVE WRITTEN to tell me that your faith is frequently tested by the slings and arrows of outrageous fortune, or just to say you are not having an easy time of it. When you are finding it difficult a sense of humor comes in mighty handy. Our Lord had a sense of humor and there are many examples in the Scriptures of the Apostles yukking it up when the going got rough.

It is during these trying times when you must lift your chin up, throw your shoulders back, and pull your stomach in. Then let out a really good laugh. A real belly laugh. After you do this a few times you will find that laughter actually comes very easily. Soon you will find that you can laugh at almost anything. Keep laughing until your knees buckle and you are red-faced and convulsed on the floor. After you pick yourself up, you will find that things don't seem quite so desperate as they did just a few minutes ago, and you can then approach your faith with a renewed vitality and sense of perspective.

MY FRIEND THE RABBI
"I can't hold it against him . . ."

IHAVE KNOWN Sidney Green as long as I can remember. Back in Brooklyn, Sidney and I would play stickball in the street, sneak smokes behind the malt shop, and try to avoid the bullyboys who forever seemed to be tormenting us. But early in our friendship I realized that Sidney and I came from different worlds.

He didn't go to our school, for one thing, and everyone I knew went to St. Anne's. Sidney also wore funny hats, even on real cold days, and I used to yell at him from down the street, "Hey Sidney, your hat ain't got no flaps!"

But the thing that really clued me in to how different we were was that Sidney used to put on his funny hat with no flaps and go to church on Saturday. Going to church on Saturday (cont'd on page 12)

BACK TO THE FUTURE
"If we could travel back in time to the days of Christ . . ."

IMAGINE, if you will, a modified DeLorean that could whisk us back through the ages and land us in any time and place we wished. This was the premise of the astoundingly successful movie *Back to the Future*, starring the new sensation of film, Michael J. Fox, as schoolboy Marty McFly. Let's suppose for a second that Marty was actually an altar boy in the film and that the scientist who created the DeLorean "time machine" was an eccentric priest. Rather than the 1950s, would it not be possible that they could have sent their amazing vehicle back to the time of Christ?!

What would Marty McFly have seen had he chosen this route to the past? Would he have used his knowledge of future events to tell Jesus his fate? Of course not! Jesus already knew what was in store (con't on page 10)

BLAKE'S LAST STAND
Why did they take "Helltown" off TV?

AT LAST, into the wasteland of television entered a "real" priest who confronted the real problems of his parish. Not a golf-playing Jack Lemmon type driving around in a BMW, but a nitty-gritty, caring soldier of our Church. Robert Blake, of "Baretta" fame, flawlessly acts this ghetto priest, and rectories all across the country were tuned in to his weekly adventures.

Catholics finally had a program, other than "Mass for Shut-Ins," to call their very own. But just as soon as it appeared, it was gone, axed by the shadowy powers-that-be in network television. Was there perhaps a more sinister motive for the demise (con't on page 13)

ENTERTAINMENT TONIGHT
CATHOLICISM AT THE BOX OFFICE

HOLLYWOOD AND BROADWAY seem to have a perennial fascination with Catholic material, and never more so than in recent years. The Church embodies all the great themes: love, death, power, mystery, redemption, and Really Bad Sins. As for sex, there's nothing more titillating these days than celibacy. A few of the following are gems of stage and screen, but the producers of most owe the public an act of contrition.

Sister Mary Ignatius Explains It All for You. Strict nun of the old school demonstrates entire range of methods for keeping present and former students in line, from rewarding them with cookies to the use of deadly force. If written today, the title character would be Sister Mary Bernhard Goetz.

Agnes of God. Mentally unbalanced young Sister Agnes gives birth to child and is accused of murdering it. Did she or didn't she? Not even Mother Superior knows for sure. Agnes says the whole thing was a miracle, but a true miracle would have been a plausible ending to this preposterous plot.

Mass Appeal. Popular but superficial priest played by Jack Lemmon learns to confront his insecurities and the complacency of his wealthy parish through the intercession of painfully sincere young seminarian. This is one version of *The Odd Couple* Lemmon should have avoided.

Brideshead Revisited. Lavish "Masterpiece Theatre" series shows Catholics at the highest levels of the British aristocracy, thereby making it worthy of William F. Buckley's commentary. Even Sebastian's teddy bear has a saint's name (Aloysius), but unfortunately is also the series' most sympathetic character.

Monsignor. Christopher Reeve plays ambitious young American priest who rises faster than a speeding bullet through the Vatican hierarchy. Film, however, lands with a leaden thud.

The Thorn Birds. Handsome young priest is tempted in the desert of the Australian outback and succumbs. Notable chiefly as the made-for-TV movie that established Richard Chamberlain as a fixture in all subsequent major miniseries.

Shogun. Richard Chamberlain (see ***The Thorn Birds***) plays English Protestant sea captain cast adrift among bloodthirsty Japanese warlords. His deadliest enemy, however, is a devious Portuguese Jesuit. So much for ecumenism.

Heaven Help Us. Indeed. With its fine cast, funny bits, and wonderful re-creation of the Brooklyn Catholic high school scene of the early 1960s, this could have been the Catholic *American Graffiti*. Instead, it turned into *Porky's Goes to St. John's Prep*. It's a shame to say, but all it needed was a little more soul.

THE YEAR IN ROMAN CATHOLICISM

1985 was a banner year for Catholics all around the world. The Pope was front-page news again, as were his bishops, who churned out a record number of letters. Here are some of the highlights:

Pope begins the year by traveling.

Fr. Andrew Greeley publishes blockbuster novel.

Bishops write a letter.

Pope travels some more.

Fr. Andrew Greeley's last novel goes into paperback and is a blockbuster.

New Cardinal for New York.

Pope travels again.

Chicago archdiocese sued for copyright infringement of hymns.

Pope forgives man who attempted to assassinate him.

New Fr. Andrew Greeley novel hits the best-seller list.

Mehmet Ali Agca, the man who tried to assassinate the Pope, says crazy things in court.

Pope ends year by traveling.

"Helltown" premieres, with Robert Blake playing the role of a priest.

Fr. Andrew Greeley does an ad for *TV Guide* article on "Helltown."

Bishops plan to write new letter.

CATHOLIC FUN FACTS

I Love L.A. The Los Angeles archdiocese knocked off the Chicago archdiocese for the largest-archdiocese-in-the-U.S. honors. L.A. claimed 2,373,021 Catholics to Chicago's 2,368,316.

FIVE

ALL THINGS VISIBLE AND INVISIBLE

THE LETTER OF FATIMA

ON MAY 13, 1917, Lucia, Francisco, and Jacinta were out taking a walk when they met a beautiful lady. She asked them to come back to see her on the thirteenth day of every month. In October, she said, she would tell them who she was and what she wanted.

Being good children, Lucia, Francisco, and Jacinta went home and told. When they returned in June, fifty people came with them. The lady appeared again, but alas, only the three children could see her. In July, 1,000 people came with them, but still no one could see her but the children. In August, 18,000 came; in September, 30,000, but not one of the spectators got a glimpse. In October, the vision announced to the children that she was Our Lady of the Rosary. This time, an interested crowd of 50,000 saw something—the sun wobbled around, twirled, fell, and then went back to normal. Two of the children died soon thereafter.

Lucia, who survived this experience, grew up and became a nun. The Pope asked her many times to tell him exactly what she had seen and just what Our Lady had said, and she did, many times.

Mary had given the children a letter before she went away. When the Pope read it, he cried for three days and then put it away. He never told anyone what it said, or whether Mary had a nice handwriting, but supposedly it named the date of the end of the world and said something about the Russians.

Periodically, rumors circulate that the Pope is about to open the letter again, but our hopes of finding out if we face imminent catastrophe are always dashed. He says there never was any letter. We know there was, and hope that its contents will be revealed in our lifetime. Otherwise, we will have to ask Mary ourselves.

What Might Be in the Letter of Fatima

1. Tomorrow's race results

2. The original formula for Coca-Cola. This is enough to make anyone cry.

3. The winner of Best Actress in a Supporting Role, 1917.

4. The winning Irish Sweepstakes ticket.

5. The recipe for a perfect martini.

THE MIRACLE OF BAYSIDE

Some people might consider the trees, flowers, and grass that grow in the Bayside section of Queens, well within the borders of New York City, miracle enough. But not Veronica Lueken, a Bayside grandmother who, for the past sixteen years, has been seeing even more miraculous things there than the rest of us have seen. In the early seventies, her entire neighborhood had to be contained behind police barricades, causing more than one startled local to conclude that Patty Hearst had been cornered. But it was not the SLA behind those police lines: It was the BVM.

Why did certain members of the Holy Family choose to visit this obscure little corner of Queens? That's what Mrs. Lueken's neighbors wanted to know. So did the parishioners and priests of St. Robert Bellarmine R.C. Church—whose front lawn played reluctant host to Veronica Lueken's weekly vigils. She ultimately was coaxed to another obscure little corner of Queens, this time in Flushing Meadow Park, the site of the World's Fair (and no stranger to mystifying spectacle), where she regularly transmits messages from Our Lady. Although thousands of people around the world believe in Veronica's visions, the Catholic Church is decidedly skeptical.

THE DEVIL'S ADVOCATE
CERTIFYING SAINTHOOD

IT WAS THREE o'clock in the morning on a Sunday and I was sitting in my shabby little office in the Vatican, sipping some leftover Communion wine and puffing on the last of my Luckies. I thought I saw a shadow pass by the smoky glass of my cracked office window, the one with the barely legible stencil, FR. SAM GUMSHOE, D.A. I kicked back my chair and took a few tentative steps toward the door. A stillness had fallen over this back corridor in the bowels of the Holy City, but then again things are always pretty quiet in this part of the Vatican—we call it the Catacombs.

I reached silently for a crozier that was propped up against the wall. (Some bozo cardinal from Wagangi left it here and I never got around to shipping it back to him. God knows where Wagangi is.) Slowly the door began to open with an ominous squeak. As I hefted the crozier, the shadow crept into my dimly lit, dank-smelling office like an uninvited guest at a cocktail party.

The door, now fully opened, revealed the outline of a man, but the hall lights blaring eerily and incessantly behind the figure made it nearly impossible to see who it was. But then, that unmistakable twinkle of the eye that I had come to know and love shot forth from the apparition's countenance and allayed my growing fears. "Oh, it's you, Your Holiness!" I gasped, lowering the crozier, which now seemed silly in my hand. "Yes, my son," he said in his pontifical manner. For indeed it was him, the man who signed our paychecks, the man we affectionately called the Jeep—John Paul II. The Holy Father.

"Your Holiness," I said. That's what I called him, Your Holiness. "Your Holiness, what brings you down these hallowed halls at this time of night?" He smiled benignly and pulled up a chair. "What are you working on, my son?" "Well, Father"—I called him Father sometimes too—"I'm looking to close the file on the tortilla thing over in the

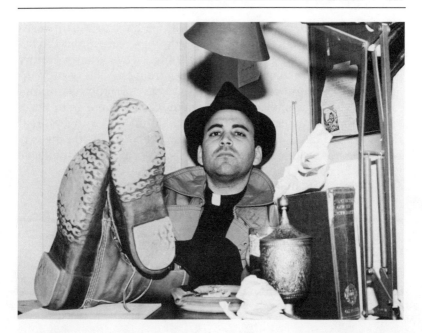

States." He knew all too well that I meant the recent claims by a pious woman in New Mexico that she had seen the face of Our Lord in a tortilla she was making. There had been some doubt cast upon her account when it was discovered that she was actually making a burrito at the time. "And then I want to check into this sighting in Montana."

He smiled benignly again and said, "Go easy on them, my son, for they have not many saints and yet have many who follow the way." With a small wave and a quick blessing he exited the office just as quickly as he had come. I returned to my cluttered desk, pushed aside the dusty files so I could put up my well-worn black shoes, and clicked off the lamp. I sat in the dark for a while. I knew His Holiness meant well, but damnit, I was a professional, and it was my job to be tough. You see, I'm the Devil's Advocate.

It is one of the toughest, dirtiest jobs in the Vatican. I investigate the claims to sainthood, and with my recent transfer to UHO (Unidentified Holy Observations) I check out reported sightings of the Big Four on earth. Although the Trinity generally is pretty easy to verify, sightings of Mary can be a lot tougher. Let's face it, it's my job to prove these things *don't* happen, not that they *do*. You don't make a whole bunch of friends at this end of the Vatican.

That's why I'm opening my

notebook on the investigation of the now-famous "Mary in Montana" sightings. The job of the Devil's Advocate is complex and important. The certification of a saint can take years, even centuries—in fact, usually centuries—and the paperwork is unbelievable. Since almost anyone who can be proven to have seen Our Lady has a shot at sainthood, we have to start investigating these cases from the beginning. What follows are my notes from the "Mary in Montana" case. In the beginning, there was the word from Bozeman, Montana, and before I knew it I was winging my way across the Atlantic on the Papal jet, *Wings of the Dove.*

Excerpts from The Notebook of a Devil's Advocate

Cruising my way across the uncharted wastelands of Montana in my rented Chevette, I reflected on my mission. It wasn't going to be my job to figure out whether the Mother of God had actually been seen in a cow pasture south of Bozeman; that was already under investigation. I had been sent to check on an application for sainthood made by a parish priest on behalf of the little child who claimed to have had the visions, and to determine if this saintly little girl was actually a candidate for one of the most exclusive clubs in the universe.

The "Little One of Bozeman," as she was called, was recently deceased and the Chief wanted me to to start compiling a file on her right away, instead of waiting for centuries as we usually do. We agreed to do the legwork at the site instead of flying witnesses to the Vatican, since air fare had been causing havoc in accounting lately.

I was told I could find the "Little One's" father at a beer-and-shot joint called the Watch Where You Step. He was a grizzled but honest-looking man of about fifty. I sidled up to him and stated my business. "You from the papers?" he said, eyeing me suspiciously. "No, no, my son," I reassured him, "from the Holy See." He stared, uncomprehending. "The Vatican," I added. "Got any ID?" he asked, knocking back what must have been one of many that afternoon. I flashed him my Devil's Advocate Badge and it seemed to calm him down. "Just the facts," I said in my most businesslike tone.

Based on an extensive interview with the father of the "Little One of Bozeman," the following notes should be checked:

- "Little One of Bozeman," born Elizabeth Mae Dirsack in Bozeman. Age at decease, 9 years.
- Claimed to have seen a "beautiful lady" in Morris Cow Pasture, May 22.
- Claimed lady told her not to go to school, but to come back to the pasture "sometime next month."
- A large crowd gathered when Elizabeth Mae returned to the pasture on June 17.
- It rained on a crowd of about twenty who accompanied the small girl.
- A man with a huge goiter was said to be instantly cured.
- The sun came out when it stopped raining.
- Elizabeth claimed that the lady told her to continue to avoid school and attend movies at every opportunity.

RECOMMENDATIONS:

Not only do I think that there should be no recommendation for veneration, beatification, or canonization, but I think they ought to lock this bunch of loonies up. As it turns out, the so-called "Little One" was not deceased, as was first reported. She had been attending a continuous weekend feature at the Bijou. The miraculous cure of the goiter was actually a minor relief of a chronic case of gout. The father, when sober, revealed that he isn't even a Catholic. The "Little One" apparently was suspended from school and made up this whole idiotic story so she wouldn't have to tell her parents.

CONCLUSION:

APPLICATION DENIED. REPRIMAND IN ORDER FOR LOCAL PRIEST.

CLIMBING THE STAIRWAY TO HEAVEN
Steps to Sainthood

- A saint must have practiced more than "common sanctity."
- A saint must have all the virtues to a "heroic" degree.
- A saint must be more than "mediocre in a nice way."
- A saint must practice mortification. Self-torture, however, is not allowable.
- A saint must reach religious perfection and this must be apparent to all around him.
- A saint must be responsible for miracles through his or her intercession.

- A saint must be venerated by the Faithful.
- A saint must be investigated by the Church through the "Devil's Advocate." This formal process has a zillion steps and takes forever.
- A saint must be "beatified" before becoming a saint. This allows the saint to be shown "religious honors."
- After enough time has passed and the record checks out, the "beatified" can be made a "saint." Holy cards are then prepared for worldwide distribution.

MR. CHRISTOPHER
THE UN-SAINT

There was recently a nasty piece of news circulating that caused many good Catholics and a number of sacred medal-makers quite a bit of distress. The story was that St. Christopher, the beloved patron saint of travel, had been demoted. Needless to say, this didn't sit too well with the millions who had worn their medals to the nub by fingering them religiously on airplane flights, or when getting a ride from Sister to the bake sale.

The problem developed when it was discovered that St. Christopher was not just one person

but a composite of several ancient martyrs. But it's not fair that faulty scholarship on the part of the Church should be held against the guy we have come to know and love as St. Christopher. That guy, of course, was the one who was sitting by the river, probably fishing or doing some other saintly thing, when a little baby came up and tried to get across the river, which began getting a little choppy as soon as the kid started across. Christopher saw the kid in trouble, hoisted him up on his shoulders, and got him to the other side where he discovered the child was really Baby Jesus, who had not yet learned to walk on water. Nice story, and besides, if St. Christopher is demoted, who is going to be the patron saint of travel?*

*Actually, there are several other contenders. St. Anthony of Padua, St. Nicholas of Myra, and St. Raphael are also legitimate patron saints of travel. There is even a patron saint of travel hostesses—St. Bona—apparently the result of lobbying by the airline industry in 1962. There is not yet a patron saint of People Express, although Patience has been suggested.

We suggest that until this whole thing is worked out, it might be better to refer to our bearded, beloved "Good Samaritan" as Mr. Christopher. Those wishing to join the fight to keep Mr. Christopher from remaining an un-saint might think about starting Christopher clubs to write nice but pointed letters to the powers-that-be. They can be reached at St. Peter's, Vatican City.

How To Become A Saint Today

1. Open a chain of chocolate-chip-cookie shops and use the profits to finance a hospital for lepers in Pago Pago.

2. Start a new order of vivacious music-loving nuns who keep a dying heritage alive by singing old Folk Mass tunes at schools and hospitals.

3. Get hit by a four-axle Mack truck and die on your way to 6 A.M. Mass. (Does not apply on Sundays or Holy Days of Obligation.)

4. Coordinate presidents, monarchs, and other heads of state in a worldwide "Bingo for Peace" tournament.

Holy Cards: Collect 'Em All

Every Catholic schoolchild remembers fondly the beautiful illustrated pictures of his or her favorite saints, which were bestowed as rewards for answering questions correctly or receiving one of the sacraments. You might get a Mary Assumption card for winning the spelling bee, for example, or a St. Francis of Assisi for perfect attendance. One could assume that if you had many of these exquisitely produced cards, frequently gilt-edged, you were a Good Catholic and getting a little closer to *Him* with each acquisition.

Yet children, being children, would sometimes trade their cards as if they were trading baseball cards. "Hey Bobby, give you a St. Jude for a Francis the Sissy and a St. Peter." Some cards became far too common in circulation and children would frequently have doubles or even triples of them. If the school was named St. John the Baptist, each child might have six or seven of St. John with his head on a plate and be eager to trade them with the kids from Ascension, who had some great ones with Our Lord up in the air on colorful clouds.

REAL LIVES OF THE SAINTS

SINCE SO MUCH of what happened to the saints took place hundreds and sometimes even thousands of years ago, much of what is known about them is subject to distortion and misinterpretation. Here are two prime examples.

ST. BERTHA

As the story goes, St. Bertha owned much of the Rhineland and married a pagan. Her husband was killed in battle and she devoted her life to raising her son as a Christian. They gave up all their land and became hermits.

What really happened is much more complex. Bertha married a huge fat man whose nickname in German was "Piggen." When he was killed at the front lines—drunk as a skunk, he ran his horse into a tree—she inherited all that land on the Rhine. Through bad real estate investments made with a group of monks who would later become Lutherans, she lost the land and retired to a small château in a remote part of Germany. There she did do wondrous and Catholic things and thus deserves to be a saint.

HUGH OF GRENOBLE

A layman who became the canon of the cathedral at Valence, he is credited with cleaning up Church corruption in his area of France by fighting simony—the buying and selling of Church favors—and reinstating celibacy for the clergy. He was granted the status of bishop and put in charge of the see at Grenoble.

What seems to have gotten lost in this story is the fact that Hugh was a terrific skier. Like our current Pope, he loved the great skiing around Grenoble and encouraged the newly celibate clergy to take up the sport, which in their day was called "sliding on snow on skinny rails of wood." By all accounts, if the Olympics had been held at Grenoble during his day, he would have made Jean-Claude Killy's performance look like Jerry Ford's. Hugh is the patron saint of the downhill.

MY FAVORITE MARTYR

by Kevin Kelly, Fifth Grade

We were supposed to write about our favorite saint. My favorite is St. Sebastian. He was a martyr. That's somebody who got killed for being a Catholic. Everytime you see a picture of St. Sebastian he is tied to a post and is shot full of arrows. A bunch of arrows. But that's not why he is my favorite saint. He is my favorite because he was a member of the Roman Imperial Guard and wasn't supposed to be a Catholic, but he decided to anyway. Also, nobody knows this but St. Sebastian didn't die because he was shot full of arrows even though the people who shot him must have been standing real close to get so many into him. After a while he got better. When the Romans found out he was still alive, they sent a bunch of soldiers with clubs instead of arrows and they beat him to death.

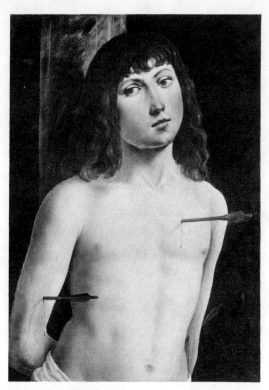

APOCALYPSE NOW

or

YOU AIN'T SEEN NOTHING YET

THE CHURCH PROMISES unmistakable signs of the end of the world, which could be any day now.

Look for giant locusts decked out like horses ready for battle, with women's hair and lions' teeth. (These should not be hard to spot.)

Look for people staring at dead bodies and refusing to bury them for three and a half days.

Look for flashes of lightning, loud voices from no apparent source, peals of thunder, an earthquake, and heavy hail.

Look for a beast that has two horns like a lamb, but which speaks like a dragon.

Look for men to gnaw their tongues in anguish and a woman drunk with the blood of saints.

(Hold the celery, please).

Look for birds to gorge themselves on the flesh of kings and an angel with the key to a bottomless pit.

Look for Jerusalem to reappear in the following dimensions: foursquare; its length, breadth, and height measuring twelve thousand stadia each. (You will need a calculator to check this.)

If you see any of these things and you are not under the influence of drugs or alcohol, you can be pretty sure the Second Coming has gotten under way. Proceed immediately to the nearest Catholic church. You don't want to be judged with any mortal sins on your soul, and the lines for the confessional will be long.

Mary Jane Frances Cavolina Meara was born in 1954 and grew up in Bayside, New York, where she attended Sacred Heart School. She was a model student despite the fact that the nuns told her that her mother would not be joining her in heaven because she's, well, you know, Jewish. Undaunted, Jane once received a prayer book for never turning her head during Mass. She attended St. Mary's Girls' High School, where she came to a better understanding of the concept of purgatory, and went on to receive a B.A. Honors degree from Hunter College. Jane is currently an editor with Beech Tree Books, an imprint of William Morrow and Company.

Jeffrey Allen Joseph Stone was born in Providence, Rhode Island, in 1955 and grew up in Westbrook and Gorham, Maine. His parents encountered some difficulty at his Baptism, when an associate pastor maintained that neither "Jeffrey" nor "Allen" was a saint's name. His position among his co-authors is unique in that he is the only "public"—a Catholic student who attended "regular" schools and received religious instruction at CCD classes. Jeff graduated *magna cum laude* from Brown University in 1977. He is a co-author of *Treasures of the Aquarians, What Color Is Your Toothbrush?*, and *The Complete Travel Guide to Thoroughbred Racetracks in the USA and Canada,* and a partner in the book production firm East Chelsea Press.

Maureen Anne Teresa Kelly was born in 1957 and was baptized at Most Precious Blood Church in Denver. Her first confession was said at St. Pius X Church in Dallas, and she received her First Holy Communion at Holy Ghost Church in Houston. In parochial school she won a glow-in-the-dark plastic Madonna for selling Holy Childhood Christmas Seals and was a member of the Junior Altar Rosary Society, an organization of young Catholic girls dedicated to straightening church pews and dusting kneelers. She went on to St. Agnes Academy in Houston and Randolph-Macon Woman's College in Lynchburg, Virginia. Since graduating in 1979, she has lived in New York. Currently, she is involved with writing projects and is a freelance publicist.

Richard Glen Michael Davis was born in 1953 and was baptized at St. Valentine's Church in Cicero, Illinois. After attending Sacred Heart, St. Elizabeth of Hungary, Mary Queen of Heaven, and Christ the King schools, he graduated from Montini High School—Montini being the surname of Pope Paul VI—and went on to receive a B.A. from the University of Illinois. He is a co-author of *Treasures of the Aquarians, What Color is Your Toothbrush?*, and *The Complete Travel Guide to Thoroughbred Racetracks in the USA and Canada,* and a partner in the book production firm East Chelsea Press. He still lives in an apartment overlooking St. Francis Xavier Church.